MW00614413

I'm not Hitler

A Real Conversation about Entry to Heaven

MIKE LYON

Artistic Lyon, LLC
3200 Main St, Unit #3.2
Dallas, TX 75226
www.artisticlyon.com
Ordering Information:
Quantity sales. Special discounts are available on quantity purchases by corporations, associations, and others. For details, contact the publisher at the address above.

Printed in the United States of America
First Printing, 2019
ISBN 978-1-7329974-0-0
Typeset by Amnet Systems.

United States Copyright
Type of Work: Text Registration Number / Date: TXu002128506 / 2018-12-21
Application Title: I'm Not Hitler. Title: I'm Not Hitler.
Description: Electronic file (eService)
Copyright Claimant: Mike Lyon. Address: 3200 Main St, #3.2, Dallas, TX, 75226.
Date of Creation: 2018
Authorship on Application: Mike Lyon; Citizenship: United States.
Rights and Permissions: Mike Lyon, mike@artisticlyon.com

CONTENTS

You're not good enough for heaven.
For real.
You got no chance.
Trust me, you'll see.

PREFACE

This is not a religious book. It is not a book about how to live a better life and make your dreams come true. It is a book about thinking through life's most profound questions. I'm not here to preach or pound or guilt anyone. My goal is to encourage a more rigorous thought process for something as serious as life and death for eternity. I talk about hard things, and I do compare ideas, and yes, discuss that cringe-inducing topic we only whisper when alone... religion. This is my provocation to anyone reading this book: ask the tough questions. In my pinball wizard mind, each chapter represents the pendulum swings of personal concerns, anecdotes, and conversations I've had. Most of the topics are my attempts at reframing established theology, and many are things I screamed at personally.

I'm on a journey, and I hope to take you on a ride that influences yours. Popcorn and a soda pop might be good for certain chapters, herbal tea for others... or a nice shot of Kentucky rye to wash down some that sting.

ACKNOWLEDGEMENTS

Many thanks to Katherine, Philip, Kevin, Trinity, Courtney, Beka, Marissa, Geoff and Byron for helping push my thoughts from swirling in *me head* to words on digital paper.

PROLOGUE

Eric and Seth, long-time friends, are having a beer at their favorite local pub, Beggars & Choosers.

"Man walks into a—" starts Eric.

"Oh no, another doomed attempt at comedy?" Seth interrupts.

"Get ready to fall off your stool, pal."

"I'm waiting."

Eric starts: "Here are three things that are difficult to say when drunk: preliminary, proliferation, and cinnamon. Here are three things that are *VERY* difficult to say when drunk: specificity, passive-aggressive disorder, and transubstantiate. There is one thing that's DOWNRIGHT IMPOSSIBLE to say when drunk: No thanks, I'm married… Bada-bing, try the veal…"

"Speaking of, how's the nuptials these days?" asks Eric.

"Man, takin' it day by day," sighs Seth.

"That sounds like more than 'all good, brother.'"

"Yep, not bunnies and sunshine at home. Rosalyn's whippin' me these past few months."

"Sorry to hear. Tell me more if I may dig a bit… Barkeep, me and my boy gonna need a couple more. Keep 'em comin'!"

Seth smiles. "Yessir, if this next round can make me Superman version 2.0… Boom, I. AM. GOLD!" he says as he flexes his chest. "We got into it *again* last night about her thinking I can't control my temper. I mean, I don't know how to act. My frustration flares up for reasons that make perfect sense. But she ain't seein' with my glasses…" he trails off.

"Like what makes perfect sense?"

"You know, like bustin' my ass at the firm! Partner track got me the big bump in pay, but it comes with expectations of more hours. I come home and don't always have my 'you had me at hello' face on."

Eric leans in. "Hmmm, this ain't gonna be easy to hear, but we've known each other for years. Take a quick shot to soften the kick."

Seth laughs. "Naw, man, speak your mind. I got my big boy pants hiked up."

"You've told me multiple times the past couple of years how Rosalyn rides you about your temper; she said you need anger management counseling."

Seth folds his arms tensely. "Look, man, I'm doin' my best! The shit ain't easy. We moved to the new house, private schools for the kids, Rosalyn wants me at every volleyball practice to encourage the girls. There's only so many plates I can spin!"

"And I heard your version of encouragement was yelling at the coach from the bleachers," Eric says, placing his hand on Seth's shoulder.

"For fuck's sake, gimme a break. I do my best to be a good guy. I try to be a good husband, do the dad thing, go to church when I can," he says, looking down.

"Tell me what it looks like to be a good guy. As in, how good?"

Seth blinks, looks at Eric.

"We say that shit all day, but what does it mean to be *good*? I mean, at what point are we sorta good but then also sorta bad? Is there like a grade? How do we measure it?"

Seth gets defensive. "Hell, I don't know. Like I said, I just do my best and figure God knows my heart. Rosalyn rides me like I'm some rotten guy. Come on, I'm no saint... but I'm not Hitler!"

1

SUFFERING IS BULLSHIT!

"But a mermaid has no tears, and therefore she suffers so much more."

—Hans Christian Andersen, *The Little Mermaid*

This world has teeth and will bite you. Grab a few drinks with five friends and ask each one if they've experienced pain in the past. Behind the veneer of competency and assuredness, you'll find buried wounds of violence, sexual abuse, and broken parenting. Maybe breadcrumbs of healing have taken place, but often the trauma has been duct-taped like a bad plumbing job.

One of the biggest challenges we face in life is to believe in a God who gives a shit about the divergent plots in our lives. In my journey, I vacillated between a God of my creation as sort of a holy executive assistant, or does

God exist at all? There's so much outright evil that goes unpunished, that I became numb and thought, "Hay-ell no! He's not involved." If so, Elvis has left the building with what looks like a big ol' middle finger to the fine folks trying to make sense of the carnage.

A minimum of three days a week I shake my head in disbelief at our fucked-up world. A recent example involved a friend opening up about her childhood. The courage it took to describe her family history astounded me. She was adopted and raised by an abusive mother. She's let me include her story below:

> I would watch her at Bible study, on the couch with my dad, and praising Jesus and talking about how the Holy Ghost moves through his flock at church. It burned me up. Maybe my head was still hurting from her dragging me down the hall and through the living room by my hair, down from their bedroom at the back of the house, where I had failed to dust a bedside table. Then from dragging me to the front of the house where the dust cloths were, while she raged at me for being so lazy and useless and craned my neck to smash my face into the cleaning bin. Or maybe I was still hot with shame after the scrubbing she gave me years earlier in the scalding bathtub, tears streaming down my face as she rubbed the washcloth angrily between my legs while telling me I was so filthy, and didn't know

how to clean myself, and maybe that's why some man had messed with me.

The year before I attempted suicide, there were two things that kept me from the deed: One, it would crush my father, and two, I would go to hell. By the time I finally gave in to the need to end my life, the desperation and hopelessness was so great, the darkness was so thick, even those massive weights weren't enough to hold me where I was. I needed relief more than I needed to be good or redeemed.

I suffered this broken but SAVED woman and tried so hard to earn her love. Through our secrets and my shame I tried to make sense of her love of Christ and complete hatred of me. I knew I was not good; obviously I wasn't. But I also had some sense of the fact that I would treat any animal more kindly. That I knew. I understood that I was unlovable, but I struggled with where the fuck was this Holy Ghost, because I wouldn't kick a dog the way she kicked me. Shouldn't he at least intervene sometime to keep a child's body safe? Shouldn't there be some evidence of his love in the people who had asked him in? I was giving blowjobs in a shower when I was three. Now I was here in a new, "safe Christian family," and it was no safer, no kinder. This Jesus, this Holy Ghost, he was NOWHERE that I could see.

God, where were you in her story!?

A visceral punch to the gut. I grapple with belief because of the struggles I hear from my dear friend above or read about daily in the news. It's a constant battle of, "What the fuck, God!? Why!? Why!? Why!?" I readily admit that knowing how the universe works is 1000x above my paygrade. A saccharine *thank you* to all the Christians who explain it away with, "Well, it's a broken world." Yep, got it, and I have read how all the heavyweights of theology through the ages have reconciled this cosmic tragedy. But the bigger frustration is directed at God as he asks me to go out into the world and sell people on a bunnies-and-sunshine fairytale of a personal relationship with this Jesus character. Too many days I throw up my hands and say, "No thanks. I don't have the faintest clue of your love language!" In practical terms, you might be thinking it's like if I had a wife who I claimed to love more than she can fathom... and then punched her in the nose and said, "Trust me, I know it doesn't make sense, but this is how I show love, it's good for you." How long would the relationship last? Or maybe you're thinking, "Hey, God, I'm drowning here! I'm going underwater and can't breathe!" His response: "Don't worry, I'm right here beside you... while you drown." Uh, gee, thanks, I hope you had a good seat! Why not send a shark for more giggles?

Trust me, I feel ya. The whole premise sounds like bullshit. Let's see if this book helps clean it off your shoes.

Questions:

1) What pain or challenges have you experienced in the world that make it difficult for you to believe there's anything more than a big, cold universe? Family history? Hypocrisy of people who claim religion or faith as a foundation?

2) What is your anchor in life that helps you navigate the daily battles that beat you down?

2

FADE TO BLACK

"I have 50 million followers on social media… My biggest fear is to die… Because I have no idea what happens after. And I'm really scared that it's nothing, because that would be beyond boring."

—Paris Hilton, *The American Meme 2018*

Have you ever felt like there was no way out of a situation… alive? When I was twenty-seven years old, I was at a low point, or at least my first genuine low point that wasn't a hangnail like missing prom or a free throw. I remember feeling behind in life, that I was already at full speed and falling deathly behind my co-racers. I kept trying to soothe my revved-up mind. "You got time. No sweat at all, you're only twenty-seven. But damn, my twenties went by fast!"

According to Ecology.com, 151,600 people die each day. The city of McKinney, Texas, is a fifteen-minute drive from Dallas, the city where I live. McKinney has a population of 144,000. Every day the equivalent of an entire city passes from this planet. Every. Single. Day.

The denouement to many a conversation is, "Death and taxes, you can't avoid 'em." An argument could be made that the latter is often bypassed to some degree, but the former is 100 percent Pittsburgh steel. There's no chance involved, no miracle cure. No level of exercise, diet, or plastic surgery can remove it from this mathematical equation: birth + life = death. Yet it's fascinating how infrequently people speak of or question the absolute certainty of this event.

As I pondered these things, I couldn't help but be amazed at how much importance society places on sporting events, parties, or concerts. We stand in line at nightclubs behind the velvet rope, hoping we can enter the latest hot destination. But when it comes to life after death, we blithely coast along without a care. Or a few of the most adventurous among us try to maximize every moment in an attempt to squeeze every ounce out of our life experiences. The adventure seeker requires ever-increasing highs to maintain the sense of accomplishment: another promotion, the next epic vacation, a triathlon, a fourteen-thousand-foot climb, maybe a shiny new spouse. Our unfulfilled lives beat us down to the point where we just lay back in our boat and float down the river, numb to the meat of life. The pretty lights on the shore distract us. Up ahead there's a waterfall. We should prepare for the impending drop, but we don't give much thought to the reality of our doom. Do we look for a captain to advise us? Perhaps the captain is a deity, and he, she, or it is warning everyone to put on their life preservers. Are we listening? Many of us choose to live in the moment with our eyes focused on the pretty distractions on the banks of the river. This book is an encouragement and challenge to spend time thinking about the impending waterfall we face; it's an encouragement to look for, question, and listen for a captain with a life jacket that could give safe passage to your next destination.

Questions:

1) Do you have an urgency about making an impact in this life?
2) How does the realization of death motivate you?

3

FOMO! YOLO! ETERNITY!

*"If we find ourselves with a desire that nothing in
this world can satisfy, the most probable explanation is that we were made for another world."*

—C.S. Lewis

In the past three years, David Bowie, Prince, Robin
Williams, Glenn Frey, Tom Petty, and Anthony Bourdain
have all died. Famous and non-famous people die every
day, to the tune of roughly 7,430 people in the United States
alone.[1] With our 24/7 connected culture and unlimited
digital content, the finality of death often doesn't fully register. Particularly with deceased musicians and actors, I can
watch them on TV and YouTube, or listen to their music
decades after their passing. We often say their legacy will
live on forever, which is true. But it can also dull the reality of death. We can develop a false sense of living forever

without contemplation of the end to this life. I'm not saying we should walk around in fear and question whether each day is our last. But we do need to urgently consider what controls we have of the outcome after this life.

According to a 2007 Pew study of religious beliefs across the country, 92 percent of Americans said they believe in a god or universal spirit, and 74 percent said they believe there is a heaven.[2] Yet our postmodern culture, with the advent of social media, is driven by the acronyms YOLO (You Only Live Once) and FOMO (Fear Of Missing Out). The idea is we must maximize every moment of life, and any inkling that we may have missed out on a super zippy experience, causes low-level anxiety and, for some, a debilitating addiction to social media. I often refer to these maxims as living out your Mountain Dew bucket list, where a person must experience life in a big, risky way, like jumping off a cliff, amped up on caffeine! After all, we only live once; therefore, make the most out of your time and don't have regrets.

In my own journey, I live in an area of downtown Dallas called Deep Ellum. It has some colorful history, is known for being edgy, and the bars and music venues buzz with a palpable energy. For years I had a consistent routine of cranking out work during the day, then Thursday through Saturday were designated days to frequent the nightlife. In the late nineties, there was a graffitied street tunnel leading into Deep Ellum, which served as an entrance to the area. I remember walking back home through the tunnel after a night out, stepping over the occasional syringe, masses of broken beer bottles, and the bulging blankets that often had an unfortunate soul or two residing underneath. The sounds of horns, music, random yelling, and other urban noise would pulsate through the tunnel. I always had a feeling of, "Damn, I hope I didn't miss anything." The thought of taking a year off from nightlife and enjoying a calming green tea or three simply did not resonate. There was no way I was going to miss whatever mystery I hoped to find. There was a tangible sense of searching for something. Maybe a feeling of connectedness?

Don't get me wrong, I'm a big fan of living passionately in the moment while pursuing people, culture, and projects. It's a difficult proposition to ask a person to suspend disbelief and trust the next life in eternity will remove all levels of YOLO and FOMO. Whuh!? No way am I gonna take that chance. I have to see, touch, smell, and hear something to believe it's real. Worse yet, what if eternity is basically a bunch of white robes and harps? No mountains to climb, no oceans to swim. What if the only beer they serve is Coors Light!? No Belgian Ales!? Egads, that ain't right. Or what if eternity is nothing but mulch? Just plain ol' dirt and zero-ness. Eww.

This skewed thinking causes a frenetic and short-sighted vision of life. My anxiety is exacerbated as the months and years fly past. As a Gen-Xer who has tried to live with a level of purposeful and healthy urgency, I can confirm this life is fleeting, and I feel the pull of FOMO.

The 2018 documentary *The American Meme* is an excellent exposé on our culture's shifting orientation to viewing life through social media lenses. The film explores several auteurs who have exploited the medium into a massive online presence. Each have millions of followers and in some cases have cultivated their content into multi-million-dollar incomes. The film also shows the dark side of the hunger for "likes." In the latter part of the movie, Paris Hilton mentions her constant FOMO, even after going out on the town for five nights a week for upwards of twenty years. She also closes the quote by saying she's scared of death because it sounds *BORING*. I wish boredom were the only concern. I anticipate her view is pervasive. FOMO and YOLO are powerful drivers, but if heaven is real, they're short-sighted maxims. They pull us into a vortex of living for now, being in the moment. Yes, please do! But don't sacrifice *ALL* consideration of the next life due to an expectation of boredom.

I recently watched the documentary *Quincy*, about legendary musician and producer Quincy Jones. He's lived an extraordinary life any creative person must respect. His level of content output is prodigious and close to unmatched. He's played, orchestrated, and produced music with Count Basie, Frank Sinatra, Miles Davis, Michael Jackson, and others. He's produced film soundtracks and musical events such as *We Are the World* and has worked with world leaders on various philanthropic projects. His list of productions goes on and on. The documentary is like watching a history of the twentieth century. And yet, his admitted workaholism has not given him a level of peace. In fact, he said he's spent his life "running from something." Granted, he used this internal fear as a driver to push his creativity and career. But he admitted his distress cost him lost years with his family and children. It almost killed him from health issues likely related to non-stop work. Is this another form of YOLO?

Personally, I have a choice when watching a documentary like this. I can see it and measure my output and career against his, which results in despondency due to the realization he's a hundred times more talented. And deep disappointment that I've missed my chance of reaching that kind of success—yes, FOMO. Or I can believe the reality that even the most staggering of artists still run into the wall of finality: there's never enough time in this world. What if in the end we just become worm food and complete nothingness? Sheesh, if I camp on that thought for too long, sheer panic sets in. I have warped thinking of, "How much coke can I snort, so I can stay up to get everything done before I croak?" Even having memorized the possible outcomes of living like Tony Montana in *Scarface*, I'm still tempted. But what if there is an afterlife, an eternity to get shit done? There is some level of comfort in knowing I may have all the time needed to achieve goals I haven't yet dreamed. Is it challenging to believe? Of course. If you see belief in heaven as wishful thinking, it might at least take the edge off your worry, and allow you to live and work diligently in the moment.

Let's look at elite professional athletes like NBA players LeBron James and Michael Jordan. The runway for the prime of their physical talent and ability is at best ten years. Jordan entered the NBA at twenty-two, LeBron at eighteen, and by thirty, their physicality started to decline. I'm not saying they were ineffective after ten years, nor am I saying their life was finished at forty (LeBron is not there yet). I am saying the decline shows how temporal our physical abilities are in this life. Pause and think about that fact. On average, most of us have fifteen to twenty years max before we begin our physical decline. *Really! That's it?* If I marinate in this reality for too long, I feel an uncontrollable anxiety building up—FOMO at the highest level.

I remember seeing a *60 Minutes* interview with NFL quarterback Tom Brady in 2009. He had won three Super Bowls by the age of thirty. In the interview, he seemed to drop his guard for a few minutes and asked the question, "There's gotta be more than this?" He was asking the bigger question many of us ponder at times. The difference is he achieved what most never contemplate. He was living out the fantasy of all fantasies: fame, fortune, and a beautiful spouse. Part of me thought, "Tom, you can't be anything but happy 24/7 every month of the year! You have it all! Women want to be with you; men want to be you! I WANT TO BE WITH YOU!" The other part of me knew deep down that Brady realizes like all of us that this life never completely fulfills. If it does, it's only for fleeting moments. The fact is, Michael Jordan, Tom Brady, Bill Gates, and Quincy Jones end up losing to Father Time like everyone else. No matter how perfect now, the most beautiful men and women will end up all wrinkly with gray hair and saggy butts and boobs.

You may think there's no way you're going to slow down your living on the off chance that heaven is real. You might miss out on something on this side of paradise. I understand the tension. However, if you haven't already realized this, you do miss out on things no matter how diligent you are with disciplined and adventurous living. I've participated in or led sixteen humanitarian aid trips to Cuba, Haiti, Africa, El Salvador, Nicaragua, India, and Guatemala. Those trips punctured my heart; they changed my worldview. I was privy to emotions I continue to process. I've also vacationed in Europe, the Virgin Islands, New York City, Chicago, New Orleans, San Francisco, and Los Angeles. And yet, I have daily moments of FOMO. I want to do more, eat more, hear more, and have my nerves wowed with exhilaration. But tick-tock-tick-tock, the years are eviscerated. Hell, I recall being blown away when hearing cultural gangster Anthony Bourdain say, "The one thing I know for sure about China is, I will never know China. It's too big, too old, too diverse, too deep. There's simply not enough time" (*Parts Unknown*).

This is a guy who had done laps around the world. He had dipped his tongue and mind into the thousands of dark alleys that scream of visceral delicacies available to daredevil souls. But again, "There's simply not enough time." Come on, if Bourdain had an inner turmoil, where does that leave the rest of us who at best make it to Disneyland for a selfie with Mickey?

Let's say a person lived an amazing and fulfilling life after being born in 1930 and dying in 2006 at the age of seventy-six. Yes, they lived through the greatest world war, saw the first man walk on the moon, and witnessed plenty of other historical moments. However, before they were born they missed the invention of the first airplane to take flight in 1903. The year after they died the first iPhone came out and revolutionized the world of technology and communication. Sure, I don't regularly wish I had been around to witness the invention of electricity; I'm not sad for missing out on events before my birth. But I do sometimes think about what it was like to see Elvis or the Beatles for the first time. I know there will be unbelievable inventions in the next fifty to one hundred years, and I will miss out on seeing them arrive in the world. As I grow older, this creates FOMO for me.

A famous prophet once said, "Why, you do not even know what will happen tomorrow. What is your life? You are a mist that appears for a little while and then vanishes." James 4:14 (NIV) Ouch! This is depressing, but true. I'm not saying you should write off living in this world cuz you're about to vaporize. Go hard, take risks, eat good meals with friends, travel as much as possible. But I encourage you to explore if there is a bigger, more important life after this brief existence here. Trust me, when you hit forty, when fifty comes screaming into sight, it's in your best interests to examine whether there's a way to extend the runway. We must consider if there is something after this *Snapchat* of a life, and if so, if there is a way to guarantee we participate in an afterlife.

Questions:

1. What's your greatest fear in life? Public speaking? Career failure? Never getting married?
2. How do you cope with the idea of missing out, whether short-term or long-term?
3. If eternity is real and includes a perfect life with the best people and exquisite meals, a perfect body and mind with no pain and no sickness, and no sense of loss, could you suspend disbelief and explore how to get there?

4

GOD? WE DON'T NEED NO STINKING GOD!

How do you define good? Do you often describe a friend in these terms: "Yeah, she's a great mom," or "He's a solid dude"? Maybe you have a small circle of tight friends you lump together in a group and say, "LOVE those folks!" There might be a next level of awesome; maybe it's a teacher, a parent you know who adopted children, maybe a community leader or pastor who seems to stand out among the crowd. We then have a Mount Rushmore of maybe Mother Teresa, Abraham Lincoln, Pope John Paul II, Gandhi, Jesus, and Nelson Mandela. We choose figures in rarified air, a relatively short list in relation to the other 7.6 billion people in the world.

Then the pendulum swings to another group, not necessarily in relation with each other, about whom we say, "Meh, they're a little shady," or, "That guy's an ass-hole, dick, douchebag…" Or add "effing" in front of the noun if you want to clarify your disdain. Personally, I describe it this way: "I'd have a beer with that guy," or the opposite, "I would never buy that guy a pint." I've had several gal pals educate me on an acronym for which I applaud and bow—possibly one of the greatest descriptions in the history of people-judging. "She has RBF," or *resting bitch face*. In other words, we're quite accustomed to making general assessments of who's good and who's bad.

In my journey, I've done the same. I justify, I say things like "God knows my heart," which is code for thinking I'm a pretty alright dude. But during my ponderings over the occasional lavender-infused, essence of cotton candy green tea, I realized my self-justification was a bit of a stretch, if not an outright farce. Am I *that* good? I can be acerbic at an Elvis Costello level. If not held in check, I can cut people with barbs that scar. Which led to the following exploration.

As we progress in our conversation, a point to clarify early in this book is a discussion I've had with multiple friends and with strangers in passing. One objection of people who are not religious is to say we don't need God or religion to be a good person. Yep, agreed. A person can have excellent integrity, morality, compassion, and work ethic, have never given the time of day to a deity, nor stepped foot in a synagogue, mosque, or church, and still be good in the world's eyes.

To begin, let's build on what appears to be a simple premise of defining good and bad.

Here are some synonyms for the word *good*: acceptable, excellent, exceptional, favorable, great, marvelous, positive, satisfactory, superb, valuable, wonderful, nice, pleasing, rad, sterling, super, worthy, admirable, congenial, honorable, precious, reputable, splendid, stupendous, and up to snuff.

Here are some synonyms for the word *bad*: substandard, poor, inferior, second-rate, second-class, unsatisfactory, inadequate, unacceptable, not up to scratch, not up to par, deficient, imperfect, defective, faulty, shoddy, amateurish, careless, negligent, miserable, sorry, incompetent, inept, inexpert, ineffectual, awful, atrocious, appalling, execrable, deplorable, terrible, abysmal, crummy, rotten, godawful, pathetic, useless, woeful, bum, lousy, not up to snuff.

Yessir, do I love me some of the *good* list. Damn straight I want to describe myself as *exceptional, marvelous, positive, valuable, admirable,* and *congenial.* For the sake of humility, I left out *honorable* and *precious.* Discarding my mom's love, maybe my friends would toss out that description if I could get them appropriately schnockered.

But here's the challenge: I *DEFINITELY* fulfill the definition of many of the synonyms for *bad.* Not even kinda sorta. I've been *substandard, inferior, not up to scratch, imperfect, faulty, amateurish, careless, negligent, inept, pathetic,* and *useless.* My ego hates me to admit it, but it's true. The reality is I'm a messy gumbo of effective and not so much. This is the premise we're evaluating in relation to being a good or bad person. For example, how would you rate yourself overall?

- Near perfection
- Very good
- Good enough
- Somewhat bad
- Very bad
- Horrible/evil

Maybe you think measures shouldn't be applied to morality or inspiration or meanness, and particularly in relation to heaven. But that's the answer I've heard 90 percent of the time in twenty plus years of asking how a person gets through the pearly gates. Try it yourself. Ask ten of your friends, "Is there a heaven, and how do you get there?" You'll receive an answer along the lines of, "I do my best to be a good person," or, "I live by the golden rule," or, "I try not to judge and try my best to show love to everyone."

I've asked this question of upwards of 100 different friends and family, and there's a consistent answer of, "Do your best to be good." Usually that's the extent of the dialogue. I've often asked a follow-up question. "Sounds nice. Exactly how good do I have to be?" There's a few seconds of blinking and confusion followed by another variation of, "I just try to be nice and not hurt anyone." If I ask a final query such as, "If there were a scale from one to 100, where's the cutoff point for being nice enough?" The discussion often defaults to the person saying something like, "Look, I'm not that bad, I haven't killed anyone.... I'm not Hitler!" In other words, the answer doesn't pertain to a measure of good. Instead we race to the bottom and pick one of the cruelest, most horrific people in the history of the world. Of course, we all score pretty well in that comparison. It's fascinating how we don't seem to look toward the heroes of mankind to base our comparison; we look to the worst first. Maybe this says something about our inherent awareness of how much of a jackass we can be.

What's Good Enough?

I have a friend, Chris, I went to high school with who created a movement called "Everybody Love Everybody." A nice title, but he puts his money and time where his mouth is and gets out there and helps people in need. For ten plus years he has asked friends and acquaintances to purchase and donate bicycles, sleeping bags, coats, and all manner of items to help the less fortunate. I'm talking about hundreds of items, every year. He dresses up like Santa Claus to deliver the items as gifts. The movement has gained traction, and several communities have created "Everybody Love Everybody" days.

I mention him because he has tangible benchmarks of impact. He doesn't simply say he's trying his best to be a good person and leave it at that. He's directly impacted thousands of people with thousands of items that helped their lives. If God were measuring his efforts against mine, I would likely fall short in that comparison. Or the comparison would get very gray when we each defined the value of our efforts. For example, I co-managed a humanitarian aid trip to Haiti after the massive 2010 earthquake. Our team delivered and converted five shipping containers into homes for five families. I also went back to Haiti in 2018 to help another group of people with unique problems. I've also been to Africa, India, Guatemala, Cuba, Nicaragua, and El Salvador, and multiple times to each country to help specific issues.

Are my efforts more valuable than delivering bicycles to kids in need? Of course, both efforts are worthy. How can anyone distinguish the value between two well-meaning people performing different acts of service? It would inevitably lead to someone feeling unfairly judged. More importantly, there is no book on earth that collectively defines the values of morality, integrity, inspiration, perfect parenting, adequate love, sufficient volunteering, charitable giving... IN THE FORM OF A SCORECARD. Yes, the Bible addresses those values, but not by the definition we're discussing here. One of my friends said, "That's the point; there is no definitive measure, God looks at each person individually." Fair enough, God looks at the person and does what? He has to evaluate, right? Would the God of the universe simply say, "Yes, you were good enough?" If he were going to judge us based on scales of measure, it seems logical he would give us the line items ahead of time. Sort of like a teacher or professor who guides and lectures the students on the subject matter before the final exam.

Many people would say people who have committed crimes and gone to jail are *bad* people. Yes, maybe they can be forgiven, and maybe they can have a change of heart. If so, then they've gotten their lives together in terms of criminal behavior. But do those blemishes on their record stop them from getting into heaven? I've been doing prison ministry for several years and have hired upwards of sixty men who have served time in prison. Most have turned their life around. If I did believe in a heavenly meritocracy, I would struggle with how to measure their life-change beyond ambiguity of non-measurable good and bad. How would I grade jail time for floating checks compared to murder? Think of Bernie Madoff. The Madoff investment scandal defrauded thousands of investors of billions of dollars. Some of his victims lost their entire life savings and had their lives ruined. Is that worse than murder? Is there a cutoff point for when felons are simply too darn bad to participate in heaven?

One of my friends replied, "Your questions appeal to people in the group who don't necessarily believe what you do. It's not about acceptance into heaven. It's about being the best we can be while we're here. In terms of each of our lists being different, that's why society matters. We communicate what we believe with each other and help each other refine our beliefs." Even our U.S. constitution has a basis in morality, and morality had to come from somewhere outside ourselves. There wouldn't be any way to refine beliefs without God who created us and our morality. If not, we would continually run into a wall of questioning which person or group has ultimate authority to validate the perfect definition of morality.

Why Does the Question Matter?

Because death is a fact. With such a significant percentage of people believing a stamp of *good* approval is all that's needed to move on after death, it seems we should understand the measure of whether there is a passing grade. I find it intriguing how reluctant—or apathetic—people are to discuss death. Unlike the subjectivity of an avid follower of NFL football or a fan of the Beatles, death is an absolute and should force us to consider what happens after the fact. I've had friends say, "Doesn't matter to me." This is an astounding response since it's undisputed... *WE WILL LEAVE THIS EARTH*. Death seems a worthy topic we can't dismiss. We don't know for sure that our final destination is complete expiration and the finality of all existence. Generally, most folks seem to assume the other possibility of heaven, where we continue life in another place or realm. Either our soul continues onward, or our entire physical and spiritual being gets transported to another destination. This view is magnified exponentially when the stakes could be a matter of eternity. If that's the case, the consideration would appear to be the most important subject a person addresses in their life: a spiritual will with infinite ramifications.

Christian pastor and writer A.W. Tozer said: "In nature, everything moves in the direction of its hungers. In the spiritual world it is not otherwise. We gravitate toward our inward longing, provided of course that those longings are strong enough to move us."[1] In response, Randy Alcorn, founder and director of Eternal Perspective Ministries, says in his book *Heaven*: "That's why we need to spend our lives cultivating our love for Heaven. That's why we need to meditate on what scripture says about Heaven, read books on it, have Bible studies, teach classes, and preach sermons on it. We need to talk to our children about Heaven. When we're camping, hiking, or driving, when we're at a museum, a sporting event, or a theme park, we need to talk about what we see around us as signposts to the New Earth."[2]

According to a 2014 Pew Research Center study, 72 percent of Americans believe in a heaven. Globally, 84 percent of the world's inhabitants, estimated at 7.6 billion, identify with a religion, according to a 2010 study entitled "The Global Religious Landscape" issued by the Pew Forum on Religion and Public Life.[3] Therefore, it's safe to assume a significant percentage of people believe in a heaven, since most religions include arrival at another destination after this life. Paradoxically, many secularists and humanists who don't believe in religion will talk about someone dying and say, "Now they're in a better place." If I asked you for the definitive path on how a person enters heaven, how would you answer? Here's my original discussion I sent to roughly twenty-five of my friends and acquaintances. Think of it like a naughty versus nice list, with God playing the ultimate Santa Claus.

Millions of people agree: if there is a heaven, entry is or should be based on some variation of being a good person as defined by not hurting anyone, treating your neighbor fairly, showing love to everyone, doing your best to be good, etc. Many people believe we can set all organized religions aside, and make heaven performance-based, essentially a meritocracy. Fair enough. Let's write out specifically how *good* is defined, with detailed metrics. Then write out specifically how *bad* is defined, again using detailed metrics. In other words, the definitions and measurements can't be ambiguous along the lines of, "I just do my best not to hurt anyone." Same as a test we take in school: we get graded, and there's a passing and failing baseline. Certainly this would hold true if we're talking life, death, and eternity. Come up with the five, ten, or twenty good things a person must do to get past God the gatekeeper. Then write out the five, ten, or twenty bad or wrong things a person cannot do, which would keep the person out of heaven. Here's a refrain I hear often: if there is a God, it's not fair that he, she, or it allows a bad person into heaven just because they say they believe in Jesus Christ. What about good Muslims, good Hindus, or the good guy down the street who has done his best?

Perhaps your answer to the definition of a *good* and *bad* person resembles this:

Definition of Good:

- Acting in the interest and service of others
- Acting selfless
- Treating people with love
- Treating people with respect and compassion for their journey and desires
- Withholding judgement
- Providing service to others without the expectation of equal reciprocation

Definition of Bad:

- Acting selfish
- Judging people
- Acting with mean intent
- Treating others with contempt
- Doing physical or emotional harm to others
- Shaming people
- Taking advantage of someone—even if no one will ever know

At first glance, the list of good seems admirable and, by most accounts, worthy of mirroring. The list of bad seems clear-cut and avoidable. However, my original discussion asks for specific metrics with benchmarks for measure.

Let's look at two of the line items: *Acting selfless* and *Judging.* To accurately measure acting selfless sounds difficult. There are days where I do act selfless and look out for others. There are a larger number of days where I'm looking out for #1, pursuing my own interests. Is it possible to apply a score to my selflessness? The same with *Judging.* I wish I didn't, but I often judge others negatively based on their taste in music, film, books, clothing, hairstyle, and on and on.

When I review the list of good values versus bad values, all appear difficult to measure in any quantifiable system. And this is only one list. Imagine hundreds of thousands of people trying to define the perfect list of good and bad values for a person to strive for each day. How many good deeds? What is the definition of a good deed? Do I have to volunteer? Do I have to donate money? What happens if I yelled at my wife ten times last year? Have I then crossed over to the *bad* list?

In addition, with the list above there are lots of items not mentioned that some people might consider crucial in defining good and bad. For example, does a person have to pray as part of their definition of good values? What about volunteering time or money to charity? On the *bad* list, what if a parent has overreacted in the past and verbally abused their child? They try not to lose their temper, but struggle with anger issues? What if the same person with anger issues has donated $10,000 every year to help homeless people? When we try to apply a measure to any of these values, we see the near impossibility of an accurate calculation. Or, when deciding the cutoff point between good and bad, is there a definitive line where a person crosses over from good person to bad person?

Do you see the futility of trying to define such a small phrase like *being good*?

When creating your list, you can't pull elements of scripture, the Ten Commandments for example. No cherry-picking of verses you like to help build your definitions. All religious texts say you gotta be all-in or nothing, we don't get to delete what we don't favor. This is the point. It's impossible to compare you and your friends with any level of good and bad with accurate metrics. Even if God could tell us exactly how much we must be selfless, how much we have to volunteer, or who is truly a good father or mother year-round, it's futile to try to measure with a truly equitable system we could fathom. The goal is to determine if there is a list that serves as a pitch-perfect definition of *good*.

On this side of heaven our lives have definitive measures, so why take a chance that eternity would have an ambiguous path for arrival? When you find you can't come up with adequate answers to the questions mentioned in these chapters, don't simply rest on, "I'll just do my best." Try defining the perfect *best,* then ask your friends and see how everyone compares.

Questions:

1. Ask five of your family and friends about how a person gets to heaven. What do they say?

2. Do you know people who have acted selfishly, judged others, treated others with contempt, and have taken advantage of others? If there were a test for heaven, would they pass?

3. How would you grade yourself if there were a test for heaven? Do you look at Mother Teresa and Abraham Lincoln as a starting place? Or do you find *bad* people to help curve your score?

4. Do you feel you score higher than your friends when it comes to morality and goodness?

5. Do you know friends and acquaintances who are head and shoulders better than you?

6. Does that make you question whether there might be thousands or even millions of people who are better people than you?

5

THE GOOD

"We men love to measure things. And we have, at our disposal, highly accurate gauges for measuring just about anything, including the progress of our lives. I mean, we never have to wonder which careers are most prestigious; which jobs are most coveted; which neighborhoods are most exclusive; which vacations are most glamorous; which cars are most luxurious. Our culture makes sure its gauges remain well calibrated."

—WIRED 2018

In the last chapter we saw that most people believe they are basically good. We mentioned a little about what it means to be good. Call it what you want, existentialism or the meaning of life, most people seek justification, basis, and intention in their lives. We use our pursuit of meaning and purpose as one of the first salvos in how we measure ourselves as good people. If we want to use a scholarly word, philosophers call it *epistemology*: the study of the nature of knowledge, justification, and the rationality of belief. This may come in the form of work and career, or family, maybe bucket list living, or an insatiable hunger for "likes" and followers on our social media channels. The basic script for most folks is we want truth and explanation for our lives to help define ourselves as good peeps. To get started on this journey, I've created three separate lists of people:

1. The Good: Individuals who achieved great things at a young age.
2. The Bad: A list of arguably the worst people in the history of mankind.
3. The Ugly: The fuzzy gray area that shows how flawed we are, every last one of us.

In this chapter we'll look at the so-called good people, the overachievers. In my experience, we often measure people based on accomplishments, not necessarily character or integrity.

The Super Achievers

1. Nadia Comăneci was a gymnast from Romania who scored seven perfect 10.0 scores and won three gold medals at the Olympics at age fourteen.

2. Steve Jobs founded Apple Computer at age twenty-one.
3. Paul McCartney was eighteen when the Beatles had their first concert, and twenty-nine when they broke up. The Beatles had written twenty-one singles reaching #1 on the Billboard Hot 100.
4. Beethoven was a piano virtuoso by age twenty-three.
5. Michelangelo created two of the greatest sculptures, "David" and "Pieta," by age twenty-eight.
6. Alexander the Great, by age twenty-nine, had created one of the largest empires of the ancient world.
7. J.K. Rowling was thirty years old when she finished the first manuscript of Harry Potter.
8. Bill Gates was the first person ever to become a billionaire by age thirty.

After reading this list, I let out several heavy sighs. I purposefully picked younger people as a measure, and displayed multiple professions and disciplines. If I do the comparison game with any of those, I can slide toward depression. If I skewed the list older to allow more time for accomplishment, maybe a Ray Kroc, who at age fifty-two helped build McDonald's into a global giant , or Clint Eastwood, who has directed award-winning films well into his eighties, I create age anxiety, as I measure how impactful or *good* I've been by comparison. Creating impact is different than being a moral person, but our culture overlaps the two. Impact from success in business, entertainment, or professional sports creates an assumption of a person's moral goodness. Many of us don't realize even a smidgen of our dreams. Our lives are not miserable, nor am I saying we're failures if we don't execute on a grandiose plan. But we do recognize how fleeting and fragile every facet of life is.

Should we give up on goals and dreams? Not at all. I'm very much a dream-chaser and map-maker. I've tried to forge my own creative path, and I encourage and applaud those brave souls who go big. My point is not to send you home weeping, but to recognize different standards for greatness in multiple fields. As we progress in our discourse, we will see how difficult it is to measure greatness or goodness.

What's the point? When measuring greatness in every field, there inevitably are champions or a Mount Rushmore of heroes. When we compare ourselves to them, we quickly have to walk back our definition of great and good. The standard then becomes, "Well, I'm not the best who ever lived, but I'm pretty good." The declaration has to be dumbed down to a small pool if I want to state, "See, compared to THESE select people, I am good."

For example, if I said I was a pretty good musician, I'm likely not Paul McCartney or Beethoven. I'm somewhere *WAY* down the list of greats, and I would likely score as average or even amateur by most standards. If I say I'm a great athlete, that's not entirely accurate compared to Nadia Comăneci. My score in the grand scheme of all-time great athletes in all sports would likely be an average score at best. If those great musicians and athletes judged me, they would be accurate in saying I'm not good, or even maybe that I'm bad in comparison to their accomplishments.

What if I'm the GREATEST scientist who ever lived?

What if I'm the GREATEST businessman in the history of paper currency?

What if I'm the GREATEST physician in modern medicine?

Is being the *GREATEST* good enough for the boss in heaven? If I were considered one of the best scientists in my field, my first thought would be, what if I'm #100 on the list, and 99 is the cutoff for greatness? What about the physician who isn't #1 or #100 but who barely made it through med school? Let's say when he or she was graded, they landed at about #4,729 on the list of 100,000 doctors. At some point, there's a delineation between the greatest scientist, businessman, and physicians; then there are the mediocre; and then the not-so-good, bordering on incompetent. The point is that we would measure their standing based on professional licenses and empirical results for these professions.

Another real-world example: Would you drive on roads that have no speed limit, no lanes, no green or red lights, and no maps? You're free to drive in your car any time you want, and you can go anywhere in the country. But you don't simply do your best. You follow the rules of the road and drive within the speed limit. If not, you receive a ticket. We live by rules and guidelines because they provide structure and order for us to excel. Everything we do in this world has value and is measured. The very definition of value requires the action of measure. Ambiguity nullifies the ability to quantify. *IF* God does judge us, wouldn't he use a system by which we're accustomed? If the eternal system is based on performance, why would a person want to bet on a definition of the game of life that has no criteria and no clearly defined formal rules? There's nowhere on this side of heaven where we lead our lives in such a way, so why take the chance for eternity?

And that's the point: We may not be as good as we think; there's lots of wishful thinking in the assessment. You may think this is all career and achievement focused, but what about being kind, loving, or gentle? For sure, these are wonderful qualities to pursue, but they are damn near impossible to measure. This also applies to tight metrics of measure for morality, inspiration, giving, supporting, judging—pick your litmus test. The goal is to help you see a bigger reality of how measures of good and bad are a tough predicament.

In the next chapter we'll look at some of the worst of the worst and how we might stack up against them.

Questions:

1. When you compare yourself to others, do you use career accomplishments as your primary measure?

2. In your chosen field, would you rate yourself in the top 100? Top 500? Is a person's profession relevant in evaluating whether they are a good or bad person?

3. If you could peer into the minds of horrible people, do you think they knew they were bad? Or did they consider themselves good people doing what seemed right to them?

4. If people inherently know what's right and wrong, is there a reasonable explanation of why people engage in bad behavior? Does our DNA appear to be broken on a global level?

6

THE BAD

*"Most people are good and occasionally do
something they know is bad. Some people are bad
and struggle every day to keep it under control.
Others are corrupt to the core and don't give a
damn, as long as they don't get caught. But evil is a
completely different creature, Mac. Evil is bad that
believes it's good."*

—Karen Marie Moning, *Shadowfever*

Theologians such as C. S. Lewis and Charles Spurgeon have
stated that the things which make us great can also be our
downfall. If I'm a charismatic leader who can inspire people to action, I may have a tendency to over-persuade and
manipulate to achieve my goals. In other words, the same
thing that takes me 10,000 feet up a mountain of greatness can travel the same distance the opposite direction in

terms of evil. Great leaders make mistakes and sometimes perpetrate horrific things.

So far we have seen the conundrum of trying to figure out the standard for good enough. In the last chapter we looked at some of the greatest in their fields and how it's impossible for most people to measure up to the Nadia Comănecis, Beethovens, or Bill Gates of the world. That is the positive spectrum of measuring up. But what about the negative spectrum of measuring up, of at least not being too bad?

Let's look at some of the worst.

The Yikes List

The New York Yankees of the 1920s had one of the greatest nicknames ever: *Murderers' Row*. This was due to their crushing ability with their bats, in a lineup that included Babe Ruth and Lou Gehrig. We're going to look at a different version of murderers' row, a list of people who committed unfathomable atrocities.

An online search brings up websites of the "Worst People in History," with these monsters on pretty much every list. I could include 500 others depending on their crimes, but the point is made by the sheer level of evil of these five. The individuals below had a magnitude of cruelty and disregard for any standard of morality, which places them at the bottom of the cesspool.

This list provides a bookend to the great people mountaintop. We can debate the top 500 and the bottom 500, but that's not the goal. I'm simply setting a baseline for astoundingly awesome people, followed by breathtaking abominable humans. The key takeaway from this chapter is for you to perform your own mini focus group with friends. Ask them a handful of questions related to how they perceive themselves in terms of *goodness*. Listen how often they race to the basement to draw their comparison. And hello, pot, this is kettle; I'm no different.

1. Adolf Hitler: He was leader of the Nazi Party and rose to power in Germany in 1933. As dictator of Nazi Germany from 1933 to 1945, he initiated World War II in Europe and was central to the perpetration of the Holocaust, responsible for upwards of seventeen million deaths overall.[1]

2. Joseph Stalin: He ruled the Soviet Union from the mid-1920s until his death in 1953. His totalitarian government has been widely condemned for overseeing mass repressions, ethnic cleansing, hundreds of thousands of executions, and famines, which caused the deaths of millions.[2]

3. Charles Cullen: He is a former nurse who is the most prolific serial killer in New Jersey history, and possibly the most prolific serial killer in American history. He confessed to authorities that he killed up to forty patients during his sixteen-year nursing career. In subsequent interviews, experts have estimated that Cullen may ultimately be responsible for over 300 deaths.[4]

4. Jeffrey Dahmer: Also known as the Milwaukee Monster, he was an American serial killer and sex

offender who committed the rape, murder, dismemberment, and cannibalism of seventeen men and boys from 1978 to 1991.[6]

5. Belle Gunness: In the early 1900s, Norwegian immigrant Belle Gunness became one of the country's most notorious female serial killers ever. She's believed to have slain over forty people in Chicago and La Porte, Indiana, including her two husbands and all seven of her children, profiting from insurance claims and other scams.[8]

You might be thinking, I know I can be selfish, but at least I'm not as bad as Hitler. When I'm honest with myself, I realize I'm much more selfish than selfless. My ambition is often myopic, only for my rewards, and I've cut corners in trying to get what I want. I've lied and stolen. I've flirted with married women, I've looked at pornography, I've had sex with women for no other reason than carnal lust. I'm not sure my supposed good deeds outweigh all the times I've been jealous, angry, and inconsiderate with my motives. In fact, what I find myself doing while writing this paragraph is immediately moving into justification mode: "I'm not that bad… I pray for people… I help people… I apologize quickly… The sex in the past was consensual, and I often said no." Yep, I quickly begin creating my own definition of what constitutes good and bad behavior. I start fudging here and there, rationalizing to make myself look better. And, boy, do I shine compared to the fab five on the previous pages. As discussed in the previous chapter, it's compelling how often people will describe themselves as a good guy or girl and say, "I'm solid, no dead bodies in the backyard."

Don't get too excited about not having too many skeletons in your closet. Every aspect of our life is measured in some way. Think of your job. All companies have employees with defined roles, deliverables, and action items to achieve those goals. If I hit my sales quota, I receive a bonus. In a healthy marriage, one spouse says "I love you" to the other, and then has tangible measures to show the value of the love. Maybe it's cooking dinner, could be roses delivered, but there is some level of measure. If the love dissipates, the measure might be the number of verbal or—unfortunately—physical fights that occurred in a year. The point is, in a job or marriage, I can't only say, "I tried my best to be good." We keep score, we evaluate, and we make determinations based on unambiguous actions. We don't measure based on heinous crimes against humanity.

I have several friends who say there are no absolute metrics for measurement, and their position rests at, "I just do my best." I created my list of answers to the original question; see below. I purposely offered tangible actions for measurement.

What if the way we defined good was to:

- Pray at least three times a week
- Volunteer a minimum of twelve times a year in your local community

- Donate a minimum of ten percent of your income every year to charity
- Go on a minimum of one humanitarian aid trip per year to help other people

And what if the way we determined a bad person was if they:

- Had sex with someone other than their spouse
- Hurt someone's feelings via a nasty comment more than twenty times in their life
- Were jealous or envious of others more than ten times in their life
- Had any felonies—even shoplifting
- Exaggerated their travel expenses or tax returns more than once

With my list, I was being partly serious and partly facetious to make a point. First, I gave specific action items to accomplish. Second, I wanted my friends to see a definitive list of bad actions to measure against. Granted, it's simply my one opinion of a list of bad things, and that too was the point. My list was not received favorably by several of my friends. They hated it! They didn't like how I seemed too stringent. They objected, "No, there can't be actual numbers or goals to achieve, plus your list is unique to you." They preferred something closer to the original list earlier in this chapter, playing a game that doesn't have definable metrics. The uproar was due to them preferring the easier method of each person being in charge of the process of determining what's good for them. They assume they can create their own list with no detailed measures; then they make a tremendous leap in hoping God will be okay with any list or description they create.

This idea of a definable list that drives us crazy brings us to the gray area.

Questions:

1. Grade yourself using measurable metrics on how good or bad you've been in your life. Were you able to create benchmarks or statistics beyond trying your best?

2. Can you name any purposeful activity that does not include measurement?

3. Can you pinpoint the exact division between the people who are just barely good enough in life, and the people who don't make the cut and are on the slightly bad side of the curve?

7

THE UGLY

"Beauty is only skin deep, but ugly goes clean to the bone."

—Dorothy Parker

While reading these opening chapters, you'll notice the entire dialogue revolves around this idea of *being good*. You could also frame the concept as a measure of value. In other words, have I created enough positive value in my life for entry into heaven? One of my friends said, "It's not about acceptance into heaven. It's about being the best we can be while we're here." The latter part is true, and I agree, but we may have action items for the former part of the statement regarding acceptance into heaven—it may not be a given. We have to ask the question of being the best at what specific metric? With sports, for example, if we measure who's the best, we look at the statistics of the athletes, as discussed in the previous chapter. If we wonder who the best salesperson is at our company, we measure total sales. There are definitive metrics. When measuring the concept of *being a good person*, should there be baseline standards to know whether we're the best we can be while here?

As we've seen the best of the best on earth, those who have excelled far and away beyond their peers for generations still might not have measured up to certain standards. And when comparing ourselves to the worst of the worst, it's easy to think we've got it made. Let's look at something a little in-between: what I call the ugly.

We're All Gray-ish

Here are several historical figures well-known for inspired and heroic work but who had various discrepancies of character. This is a good exercise in seeing how the so-called best of us made mistakes and had cracks in their armor. This helps us see our inability to maintain good character or virtue over the course of a lifetime. We make small blunders, minor misjudgments, we say things we regret later, or, in some cases, never recognize the impropriety and harm of our actions and words.

10,000 Feet Up and 10,000 Feet Down

1. Martin Luther King Jr.: A Baptist minister, an activist, and an orator unlike the world had ever seen before, Dr. King became the face of the civil

rights movement and one of the most respected leaders in U.S. history. However, in his personal life he allegedly had numerous extramarital affairs.[1]

2. Winston Churchill: He's one of the most famous men from England, the prime minister during World War II who led the Allies to victory. As prime minister he deliberately diverted food away from India to feed Europeans at a time when India desperately needed it.[2]

3. Mahatma Gandhi: An activist who preached love and peace, Gandhi led India's independence from Britain. But Gandhi had a reputation for sadism toward his children and wife, Kasturba. Gandhi condoned the Holocaust, was not a Nazi, and actively opposed Nazi plans. However, he praised Hitler, saying, "He wasn't as bad as people made him out to be."[3]

4. Marie Curie: Curie won the Nobel Prize for her work in discovering and coining the phrase *radioactivity*. However, she failed to acknowledge the possible dangers, even after ten years of several colleagues dying of leukemia after exposure to radiation.[4]

5. Flannery O'Connor: Known as the premier writer of Southern gothic fiction, O'Connor also had a propensity for making racist jokes to a friend who was deeply devoted to civil rights.[5]

6. Thomas Jefferson: While Jefferson penned the heroic and oft-quoted part of our Declaration of

Independence, announcing the "self-evident" truth that all men are "created equal," he owned some 175 slaves.[7]

7. Albert Einstein: Einstein had these written conditions for his wife:

CONDITIONS

A. You will make sure:

- my clothes and laundry are kept in good order;
- I will receive my three meals regularly in my room;
- my bedroom and study are kept neat, and especially that my desk is left for my use only.

B. You will renounce all personal relations with me insofar as they are not completely necessary for social reasons. Specifically, you will forego:

- my sitting at home with you;
- my going out or travelling with you.[8]

Yep, these folks show how how we're all kind of gray-ish. We all have some bad or at least not so good we try to sweep under the rug. In my journey, I find this to be a daily occurrence.

So far, I've given you three lists of people: outstanding people, horrible people, and great people who were not perfect 24/7. We can view these individuals as the top and bottom of greatness and pure evil and can reasonably conclude most of us fall somewhere in the middle. We're not incredible, heroic, or memorable for timeless achievements, but we're also not evil, murderous, or despicable. So how should we think about good and bad?

Money

I've often fallen into the trap of thinking if I can just achieve a certain financial threshold, I'll feel better about myself. This false comfort tricks me into thinking I'm good, because look at the money I'm making. Aren't good people blessed and bad people cursed? Don't good people hold powerful positions and make bank, while bad people live in squalor and go to prison? To a T what I've found is I lose my edge when there's money in the bank. The hunger to push, the desire to learn, is slightly diminished, and I settle into comfort. Don't get me wrong, the challenge of a career and achieving goals are worthy things to pursue. As are periods of rest to recharge and recalibrate. But if my desired outcome is "to be comfortable," I will undoubtedly miss the meaning derived in the process. Chasing comfort is fleeting at best, plus the end outcome—if achieved—will not derive any level of hardened truth. This can result in a mediocre vision of *being good enough*. In their book *Geezers and Geeks,* authors Warren Bennis and Robert Thomas talk about the crucible all leaders face: an event or circumstance that forged them and made them who they are. Winston Churchill for example, led Great Britain during a time of tremendous worry due to WWII. You might think his leadership would absolutely qualify as a heroic quality that earns his spot in the afterlife. Part of me agrees; he created hope for millions of people, he didn't cave under the pressures of war. My concern is I haven't done anything close to his level of leadership! If heroic deeds are the measure, Churchill will enjoy eternity based on merit; but I'll have to pray there's a pass given for men like me who led a rather benign life.

Integrity

Someone may say the amount of money we earn is not the point; it's a matter of whether a person has worked with integrity during their lives. As a measure of being good, we face another dilemma of how to measure standards of work. For example, could God place a sensible value in comparing Senator John McCain and his heroic chapter as a POW in Hanoi? Or Harriet Tubman, the American abolitionist who escaped slavery and helped rescue enslaved people, family and friends, forming the Underground Railroad? Could God compare them to a CPA who works diligently in a small town in Michigan? Maybe you think God simply looks at all three and deems them acceptable, in essence saying they're *good enough*. Here's the challenge with this idea: at some point, possibly between person 4,007,635,327 and person 5,088,784,000, God would have to declare a line in the sand between narrowly passing as good, and a teeny bit on the bad side to not make the grade. No doubt there would be an unfair delineation.

Most of us don't see ourselves as *bad* people. The bad people are others…like criminals in prison…or the *jackass in accounting*…or other people who don't like the same music as me. Then I thought, what if it turns out all us normal, everyday folk are slightly more flawed than we realize? No, I'm not saying you're horrible and evil, I am saying you're not as angelic as you think. Yes, you'd likely say, "Of course, no one said I was perfect." Exactly. When we humble ourselves, we recognize we're sort of average in terms of personal worth and altruism. This idea leaves the door open to the possibility of a person being below average and not quite as good as their fellow humans.

For example, at a wonderful local homeless shelter in Dallas called the Austin Street Center, one of their staff members mentioned she has to be patient with people who take selfies while serving those in need. She appreciates the fact that they showed up, but was their heart truly in it to help, or just to generate a bunch of "likes" for self-aggrandizement?

Kindness

Some people look at the Golden Rule as the end-all be-all. Are we always kind to strangers? Or only kind to the people we like, or to the people we deem worthy or valuable? I'm often impatient with people who don't agree with my opinions. Am I then living by the Golden Rule? Only when I like the people, but not if they disagree with me. I have to be brutally honest in evaluating my positions. The more I evaluate my attitudes, the more I would call them antics or charades if I look at them on a thirty-year continuum.

Law-Abiding

Here is another example: What if I've been to jail for stealing? Some people would say anyone who has been to prison is a bad person, therefore they don't make the heavenly cut. If the idea sounds crazy, ask a convicted felon how difficult it is to find a job or an apartment to rent. I have a friend who says society and our conscience determine if we can come back from our mistakes. I agree in terms of being able to rebound. He said, "The person did the time society dictated, and they deserve to be given another chance." I agree again, but I'm talking about the final authority on forgiveness. This assumes God is a forgiving entity. Without a God who forgives, in this exercise we're all betting we've been good enough and don't require any forgiveness for our mistakes large or small. Or our pride tells us we can forgive ourselves. We can, and forgiving ourselves is a healthy goal. But I'm referring to a metaphysical cleansing of the soul that we're incapable of due to the level of our paygrade. We're not magical beings with superpowers capable of deleting the ramifications of our mistakes.

The Scales of Justice

One of my friends who attempted to answer the original question of creating a good list and a bad list said: "There isn't a list of bad things that keep you out of heaven. It's inherent that if I don't do the good things, then I've created my own list of bad." This led to a discussion of what happens when I don't live up to my list of good acts or characteristics.

We often look at our mistakes as solely a mistake, and hope the mistake doesn't define us as bad people. That same friend also couldn't define a measurable list of good things.

Do you see the conundrum? We end up dumbing down our mistakes as sort of careless, maybe inadequate, but definitely not horrible. We point at others as the genuinely bad eggs. Of course, I believe there's a significant difference between a white lie and robbing a bank. My point is that we're disingenuous when we measure ourselves against others.

This exercise distills down into an idea of scales: Does the amount of good things I've done outweigh my bad things? I hope I did enough with an ambiguous list that may not line up with God's metrics. In other words, I hope I made the cutoff point between the good people and bad people. I hope the bad people are those who have served time in jail, and I hope the definition of bad doesn't include judgmental people, or those who have cheated on a boyfriend or girlfriend, or people who have lied more than 100 times in their lives—because that might be me! I hope God overlooks the time I fudged a bit on my tax return. I hope I was nice enough and invested enough back into my community, in comparison to the pastors I know who moved out of the U.S. and committed their lives to helping the poor. I hope my own made-up list is more valuable than the doctors and nurses I met on Mercy Ships who spent nine months out of the year volunteering on a hospital ship. I'm probably not as good as them, but at least I never killed anyone.

A friend said: "I think the example about overseas giving sounds incredibly thin. Society recognizes those shining lights who are serving on Mercy Ships. There's also a long list of people who are doing just as much as those examples you share, who have nothing to do with religion. They're inspiring the people in this world to be good people today, so they can then inspire others as well. Society makes the world a lot harder on you when you make bad decisions. It's a daily consequence."

Well said. I agree.

But let's include a measure of our daily mistakes, and include items like fits of momentary anger, snarkiness that hurts a person's feelings, road rage, jealousy, and passive-aggressiveness. The numbers scale quickly. Let's be generous and say you only enact two mistakes every day. Here's the math:

- Two mistakes per day x 365 days in a year = 730 minor mistakes a year
- Let's use 50 years of average adulthood x 730 minor mistakes = 36,500 errors in my life
- As of 2018, there are 326,766,748 people in the United States
- 326,766,748 x 36,500 mistakes = 11,926,986,302,000

In other words, in one year alone we can amass nearly 37,000 mistakes, and in an average lifetime all the people in just the U.S. hit a whopping twelve trillion mistakes.

Does your list of personal morality with items such as, "I did my best to treat people nice, and I volunteered at the food shelter a few times this year," outweigh the numbers above? If the claims of Christianity are true, those are just the tip of the iceberg for the metrics God is using to evaluate. Even if your ledger lined out at 38,000 positives versus 36,500 mistakes, you're still counting on meritocracy being the rules of the game. However, it's impossible to measure the scales of justice.

Any individual living by their own list or definition of good and morality must wrestle with this rigorous test. Does my list outweigh more *good* than what Christ did on the cross? Meaning, when someone says they tried to love their neighbors and all their family and friends as best they could, does their metric show more value than the measurable love of dying on a cross for all a person's mistakes? If Christianity is real, that will be God's response to anyone with their list of good deeds: "Christ died for 11,926,986,302,000 mistakes. Did you?"

A dear friend of mine thinks this is the answer:

"If you are not using your time on earth to also inspire other lives, you are wasting your time on earth. Be a bigger part of the world in some way. Some people are not. They don't think of the world outside of their immediate place in it. Make your soul matter. So there you have it. I just don't believe there's a Rubik's Cube answer to all this. Some simple life principles, done with specific actions, are how you either stay in or out (of heaven). In my mind, the kingdom of Heaven is a crowded place, and God's okay with it."

I completely agreed with everything he said. I do want to inspire others. I don't want to waste time. I want to be a bigger part of the world in some way. The problem again is what do I do with those 36,500 errors? Where is the cutoff point between my annual mistakes in comparison to those dreaded *bad* people I can't exactly pinpoint?

When I pressed one of my friends to give me firm metrics of evaluation, as in the number of times I must volunteer every year, he replied: "There are no metrics, but there are none with Christ, either. Live as a devil on earth, admit your wrongs at the end, claim Christ as your savior, and you're good. And that's supposed to make you more valuable than a person who's lived a life of being good?"

He seemed to have a point. Just believing seemed like too easy a way to erase all our mistakes. It seemed unfair that a person could run rampant in their life, make all manner of terrible choices while harming others, and then at the last moment ask for a "get out of hell free" card by accepting Christ as their savior. However, I thought, if everyone has the same opportunity to receive a free gift, how fantastic that even the worst of the worst can be forgiven.

I've had many people tell me there are famous martyrs throughout history who died for a cause bigger than themselves. Absolutely true. Martin Luther King Jr., for example; he was murdered and became a martyr. We now show our humble respects via an annual national holiday. Nelson Mandela is another heroic figure who stood for what's right and has his rightful place in history. However, do we worship either of those fine gentlemen as religious deities who have laid on the grenade for every misstep we've made for our entire lives?

Maybe a person says they don't want to believe Christ actually sacrificed his life for all of mankind's mistakes. But they'll still have to circle back to who's the manager of mankind. If the final authority is God, and his Son Jesus Christ is part of the Trinity, then a person with their personal list of good deeds may find themselves in an insurmountable game of comparison.

Jim Jones, David Koresh, and Marshall Applewhite would all tell you their deaths were a God-like offering for humanity, as opposed to the abomination they truly were. Many people throughout history have died and claimed to have given of themselves like Christ. It's Christ's intent and his proclaimed and literal resurrection that make him one of a kind, a complete anomaly in the history of mankind. He's the ultimate accountant with a ledger erasing all debts.

You may be asking, "Who cares! Why does this matter?" The answer is due to the consequences of the decision. If we're talking about whether I choose this year's Oscar winners, the repercussions in my life now and in the future are utterly irrelevant. But we're talking about eternity, a timeline that goes on forever. If eternity is real, the process and decision on getting there is *THE* singular choice in a person's life. We place utmost importance on settling our earthly matters here in the form of the weighty sounding document: our last will and testament. A spiritual will seems exponentially more important for how we spend eternity.

You may be flabbergasted at this point. If that's the case, forget all the other good or bad people. Write me and tell me exactly where the cutoff point is for the "almost-good-enough-but-didn't-quite-make-the-cut" population. Maybe it seems easy to say the bad people are those who committed crimes, molested children, judged others, and were selfish. Go a step further and see how you measure friends and acquaintances who don't exactly inspire, only volunteer once a year, or are wishy-washy with consistent integrity. The point is, all lists are arbitrary at best. And for damn sure you aren't one of those bad people, right?

In the next chapter, we'll look at the idea of an absolute moral list. Is there such a thing? Or maybe I'm blowing smoke to make you think you need a crutch to make it to heaven.

Questions:

1. Do you know people who describe themselves as not good, who would never qualify for heaven?
2. Are there areas in your life where you know you're a bad person? For example, do you become easily angered or struggle with jealousy?

3. If you measured yourself against all 7.6 billion people in this world, are you confident you'd land near the top 100 million? Where would you say is the cutoff point for those who don't make the grade? The bottom one billion? Higher? Lower?

4. Can you name a historical figure, other than Christ, who had greater impact in terms of forgiving mistakes? Is there anyone who made similar claims who has stood the test of time?

5. Why haven't we created services every week to worship Abraham Lincoln, Mahatma Gandhi, and Martin Luther King Jr?

8

NO ABSOLUTE TRUTHINESS

"Men occasionally stumble over the truth, but most of them pick themselves up and hurry off as if nothing ever happened."

—Winston S. Churchill

When I thought about the concept of the good, the bad, and the ugly, I knew that truth has to be part of the equation. Why? Because more than ever we live in a world where there's an onslaught on the idea, particularly with the recent pandemic of people labeling tried and true things as "fake news." Whether we acknowledge the journey, at one time or another everyone is seeking truth in their lives. Or if they are fans of Stephen Colbert, they lean toward a general "truthiness" in life. Colbert was brilliant in his fictitious depiction of a commentator agreeing with politicians as they edged toward almost-but-not-quite truth. As I reflected on this, I realized there are lots of people in our postmodern culture who live with a quasi-truthiness. We like to say, "My truth works for me," or, "What's right for you might not be right for me." This made me lose sleep at night, because what if someone's innate right was to scorch me off the face of the earth?

> In two national surveys conducted by Barna Research, one among adults and one among teen-agers, people were asked if they believe there are moral absolutes that are unchanging or that moral truth is relative to the circumstances. By a 3-to-1 margin (64 percent vs. 22 percent) adults said truth is always relative to the person and their situation. The perspective was even more lopsided among teenagers, 83 percent of whom said moral truth depends on the circumstances, and only 6 percent of whom said moral truth is absolute.

In other words, 64 percent of adults and 83 percent of teenagers say your truth is yours, mine is mine.

In the last thirty years, the debate of absolute versus relative truth has gained steam again. For centuries, there were certain inarguable facts and truths. The difference between the two is subtle but unique. For example, gravity is an absolute fact. If I hold my car keys in my hand and then drop them, it's 100 percent absolute fact those keys will fall to the ground EVERY. SINGLE. TIME.

There's no place on earth where the keys will magically float one out of ten, twenty, or 100 times. There's no special cliff or bridge I can leap from and magically break the laws of gravity and float. C. S. Lewis in his landmark book *Mere Christianity* goes into rigorous detail around the idea of absolute truth and morality. He describes gravity as an absolute truth: "As a body, he is subjected to gravitation and cannot disobey it; if you leave him unsupported in mid-air, he has no more choice about falling than a stone has."[1]

In his watershed book *The Road Less Traveled*, M. Scott Peck says:

> Truth or reality is avoided when it is painful. We can revise our maps only when we have the discipline to overcome that pain. To have such discipline, we must be totally dedicated to truth. That is to say we must always hold truth, as best we can determine it, to be more important, more vital to our self-interest, than our comfort. Conversely, we must always consider our personal discomfort relatively unimportant and, indeed, even welcome it in the service of the search for truth. Mental health is an ongoing process of dedication to reality at all costs.[2]

When I read this, I found myself agreeing with Peck. The search for truth really does supersede all other interests, even when it makes me uncomfortable. We often try to avoid discomfort, but, just as exercise can be uncomfortable but worthwhile, Peck is saying our mental health benefits from the search.

This got me thinking about mathematical truths such as 2+2=4. It's always four. Always. It never deviates; there are no variations where sometimes we arrive at seven or nine or twenty-six. Now, I'm not a scientist, but when I look at the periodic table I see absolutes. Element classifications that are unchanged. There's no fluctuation with H_2O. Each water molecule always has two atoms of hydrogen and one of oxygen. Water molecules don't sometimes consist of four hydrogen and seven oxygen atoms depending on their mood or time of the year. It's the same today, tomorrow, and ten years from now. Unchanging. The periodic table, therefore, is a fact, and could be argued as an absolute truth at all times and in all places. It's something that is true no matter what the circumstances.

When I thought about the idea of truth and someone having their own truth, it reminded me of the idea of *being good*. Is it really all relative I wondered? When someone says, "You live your truth, and I'll live my truth," it sounds like they are being inclusive. That's well and fine, I thought, until those truths contradict each other. But they can't. If everyone creates their own version of the truth, inevitably one or more explanation will diverge and contradict the other. Two contradictory things can't both be true. Either both are wrong, or one is right and one is wrong, but they can't both be right. It was hard for me to get my head around this, but it seemed like someone saying a person is both dead and alive at the same time. It's not possible. Regarding the existence of God, this becomes very important when discussing whether God is real, and how multiple truths play out with the major religions (see chapter 16).

You might ask, "So what?"

So did I, but I got to thinking that this idea of an absolute truth is relevant in the matter of life and death. If I declare that death is not important to me, it's like announcing the heat of the desert doesn't affect me. Guess what? The sun overrides my feelings and belief and will absolutely fry my ass, no matter how strongly I feel otherwise. The same applies to death. No matter how entrenched my apathy is toward it, I can't escape it, and I can't simply take for granted a pleasant outcome after death.

I couldn't shake that, and so I realized that one person could say there is clear evidence of God as a creator. Another person could say there is clear evidence there is no God. Neither can be considered an absolute truth unless we can empirically prove one position over the other. I can adopt one position over another and claim it as my truth. Does this mean both positions are true? No, I reasoned because the positions contradict each other. Therefore, either both are false, or one is true, but both can't be true. Maybe there is a preponderance of evidence for one side or the other, but no one can 100 percent guarantee that their truth is absolute. I wrestled with this idea and realized I would have to take a small step of faith and bet that God is real and absolute if I wanted to find out more. The alternative just didn't look promising to me.

When I looked at our culture, however, I knew it was unpopular to take a position on certain subjects without being accused of being intolerant. This was relevant in my thinking about whose definition of truth and *being good* is accurate and correct. For example, when discussing same-sex marriage, the lines are divided. If a person says they believe marriage was intended for a man and a woman, they are accused of being exclusionary and unaccepting of all definitions of love. Keep in mind that the person who points fingers and takes a firm position saying all definitions of marriage should be considered has also taken a position of intolerance toward the group who differs with his or her position. This is when I came to the conclusion that moral pluralism is not real-life. If genuine pluralism were accurate, all positions and viewpoints on those hot-button issues would be acceptable and there would be no emotional pushback. In other words, two plus two would sometimes equal nine, and on certain Tuesdays in the spring it would equal forty-seven, so who cares.

Another example that made me question this idea of all truths being equal is racism. Unfortunately, there's a significant percentage of the population who still believe certain skin tones are signs that some people groups are superior or inferior to one another. Yes, this is outright lunacy. The reality that most of the population vehemently disagrees with racism showed me that pluralism isn't acceptable. In other words, if we did believe, "Your truth is yours, and mine is mine," why do we have visceral reactions towards racism? Shouldn't we respond with a, "Great, have a nice day!" or a neutral response at best?

Then I thought about a woman's right to vote, abortion, infanticide, and even cannibalism. Depending on the culture you grew up in or where you live in the world, you may respond with outrage on either side of those issues. The outrage is proof of genuine pluralism not being acceptable. You might think like I did that obviously cannibalism is wrong, and, if so, then maybe the other things are too.

This gets very interesting when we read the Bible verse John 14:6 (NIV): "Jesus answered, 'I am the way and the truth and the life. No one comes to the Father except through me.'" Nope, when I read this I didn't fall down on my knees and repent, but it did add some spice to the queso. The verse is essentially saying Jesus is the glue that holds everything together. You could say he's claiming to be both fact and truth. I had read enough to know that even atheists concede the fact Jesus Christ was a historical figure. In the same way few people dispute whether George Washington actually existed, most reputable historians agree Christ was an actual person who truly lived. Therefore, Christ is a fact as a historical figure, but he may not be an absolute truth. Unless, it turns out that we, the earth, and everything in it, including emotions, wine, love, science, air, dirt, and rain, are pieces of a puzzle—the facts—that he's holding together as the absolute singular truth.

Another question I had regarding pluralism is whether a person's version of truth is powerful enough for people to change their lives. I thought of Nike's thirtieth anniversary *Just Do It* campaign. Colin Kapernick had taken a stand for what he viewed as unfair treatment of African-Americans by law enforcement. I applauded his moxie and love that we live in a country that values a person's freedom to respectfully protest an issue. This is exactly what makes our country outstanding. But will his cause change lives for more than two thousand years, or will he just be a footnote in history? That is the level of magnitude I was thinking about when I was pondering absolute truth versus just my own truth—or Colin's truth.

Here's another way I looked at the idea of one truth for all, or multiple truths for anyone. If I woke up tomorrow and declared I am God, and I am the path to heaven, would my so-called truth stick? Let's say I have a magnetic personality, tremendous charisma, I'm a brilliant marketeer, and I appeared on major media outlets proclaiming my deity. Would people drop everything and claim Mike Lyon as the catalyst for life change? Would we reset our calendars to say BL and AL (Before Lyon and After Lyon)? Would people 2,000 years from now still be worshipping me? It sounds ridiculous to even consider, let alone call it truth. Maybe it's not all relative. Maybe there's an alternative.

Questions:

1. Do you have significant weight, authorization, and moxie to have your own version of truth that can stand alone?

2. What do you use as a standard of truth to guide your actions? Your friends? Culture? Books other than the Bible? How do you confirm they're accurate?

3. Can you think of examples of contradictory positions that are both true?

9

I'M SPIRITUAL, NOT RELIGIOUS

"And out of that hopeless attempt has come nearly all that we call human history—money, poverty, ambition, war, prostitution, classes, empires, slavery—the long terrible story of man trying to find something other than God which will make him happy."

—C. S. Lewis, *Mere Christianity*

At this point you may think the evaluation of all this good and bad stuff isn't relevant because you don't believe in organized religion, you're more of a *spiritual* person. In our postmodern culture, spirituality is a common choice. To my understanding, being spiritual is not about religion, it's a matter of mindfulness and enlightenment. Instead of adopting one of the major religions such as Islam, Judaism,

Hinduism, Christianity, or Buddhism, people take a stance as a spiritual person. This sounded good to me, because I'm not one for following a stodgy set of rules, but I had questions. Based on my research, there are no founders, prophets, or disciples within the spirituality movement. There's no formal doctrine or guidelines to review, study, or compare. A spiritual person essentially creates their own belief system and says, "Your truth is yours, mine works for me."

As I contemplated being spiritual rather than religious, I came across my first hurdle. How does each person reconcile their beliefs when their definition doesn't match another spiritual person's definition? How do they decide who's right? What if I'm a part of a big cultural and spiritual movement, but the movement includes a controversial issue other people dislike? The people in one spiritual group share the same values, and feel they're accurate with their beliefs. They're inspiring each other, they believe in something, they think they're a force for good. But the other group disagrees and thinks *they're* inspired, and a spiritual force for good. I might think both groups are wrong according to me, but to what am I comparing them, other than my opinion?

With spirituality, there's no organized body, no formalized doctrine, no designated leaders for a person to confirm they're pursuing accurate truth. It would seem there should be a loftier final authority to confirm validity.

Consider Deepak Chopra, who is an Indian-born American author, public speaker, alternative medicine advocate, and prominent figure in the New Age movement.

Through his books and videos, he has become one of the best-known and wealthiest figures in alternative medicine. Chopra believes that a person may attain "perfect health," a condition "that is free from disease, that never feels pain," and "that cannot age or die." Seeing the human body as being undergirded by a "quantum mechanical body" composed not of matter but of energy and information, he believes that "human aging is fluid and changeable; it can speed up, slow down, stop for a time, and even reverse itself," as determined by one's state of mind. Chopra has likened the universe to a "reality sandwich" which has three layers: the "material" world, a "quantum" zone of matter and energy, and a "virtual" zone outside of time and space, which is the domain of God, and from which God can direct the other layers. Chopra has written that human beings' brains are "hardwired to know God" and that the functions of the human nervous system mirror divine experience.[1]

His bio reads like a person who would be considered authoritative within the New Age movement. He appears to acknowledge God as the fabric or force holding the reality sandwich together. But the idea we can "attain perfect health" and "speed up, slow down and reverse aging" seems to be a stretch based on existing data. In other words, we can get wonky and nerdy and say, what is the statistical significance of human aging being reversed?

"Statistical significance helps quantify whether a result is likely due to chance or to some factor of interest," says Tom Redman, author of *Data Driven: Profiting from Your Most Important Business Asset.* When a finding is significant, it simply means you can feel confident that's it real, not that you just got lucky (or unlucky) in choosing the sample. No matter what you're studying, the process for evaluating significance is the same. You start by stating a null hypothesis, often a strawman that you're trying to disprove."[2]

In everyday Joe Schmoe terms, the null hypothesis is the question of Chopra's saying a person may attain "perfect health," a condition "that is free from disease, that never feels pain," and "that cannot age or die." Is there any evidence—or statistical significance—to prove there are people who are no longer aging, and are in fact getting younger? I'm not referring to someone who exercises and maintains their health and has a vibrancy to them that gives them a youthful vigor. I'm referring to what Chopra says in terms of the fluidity of human aging, and that it can be reversed. Sort of a *Benjamin Button* thesis. This idea sounds like nothing more than wishful thinking based on existing data.

Chopra's ideas are simply one definition of spirituality. Yes, Chopra may be recognized as an important voice in the spirituality movement. Close friends of mine have made positive changes and been inspired by his books. However, regardless whether his books are bestsellers and make people dig deep into the New Age universe, we have the question of whether this definition of humanity is an accurate depiction, or just another shiny object to chase. In other words, can a person say they don't believe in organized religion, but do believe the writings of Deepak Chopra are a path to heaven? Will his writings and positions have longevity, and will he be remembered fifty to 100 years from now? He's by far more memorable and famous than me, but I know for a fact I have nothing to do with affecting the afterlife, and I doubt Chopra would say he does either. If it sounds like I'm picking on Chopra's spirituality, well, I guess I am. But I question everything, and, by all means, I implore you to ask the same question of all religions.

Some people will answer that their spirituality doesn't require a God and that the universe or nature is the governing authority. Possibly. But who's really to know, especially if there are contradicting definitions and beliefs within their spirituality. Unless the universe has provided a reference guide, the circles keep spinning with no finality for reference.

Another spiritual guru I investigated is the Dalai Lama. Tenzin Gyatso, the fourteenth Dalai Lama, is now eighty. The official Dalai Lama website, DalaiLama.com, says:

> He advocates the cultivation of warm-heartedness and human values such as compassion, forgiveness, tolerance, contentment and self-discipline. He says that as human beings we are all the same. We all want happiness and do not want suffering. Even

people who have no religious belief can benefit if they incorporate these human values into their lives. His Holiness refers to such human values as secular ethics or universal values. He is committed to talking about the importance of such values and sharing them with everyone he meets.

Secondly, as a Buddhist monk, His Holiness is committed to encouraging harmony among the world's religious traditions. Despite philosophical differences between them, all major world religions have the same potential to create good human beings. It is therefore important for all religious traditions to respect one another and recognize the value of their respective traditions. The idea that there is one truth and one religion is relevant to the individual practitioner. However, with regard to the wider community, he says, there is a need to recognise that human beings observe several religions and several aspects of the truth.[3]

Please hear me: the Dalai Lama sounds like a wonderful man. His goals and influence for his people and mankind are reverential. He's the undisputed leader and main solidifying force of the 150,000-strong community of Tibetan exiles, which is becoming increasingly politically fractious.[4] He's referred to as His Holiness, but the Dalai Lama considers himself to be "a simple Buddhist monk. I feel that is the real me. I feel that the Dalai Lama as a temporal ruler is a man-made institution. As long as the people accept the Dalai Lama, they will accept me. But being a monk is something which belongs to me. No one can change that. Deep down inside, I always consider myself a monk, even in my dreams. So naturally I feel myself as more of a religious person."

He doesn't claim to be a deity, but he "seeks to reach a state of nirvana, following the path of the Buddha, Siddhartha Gautama, who went on a quest for Enlightenment around the sixth century B.C.. There is no belief in a personal god."[5]

The Dalai Lama's intentions and purposes are marvelous, and his stance on human rights is one we should all adopt. But he's not a path to heaven, nor is he claiming to be an option.

So I looked at two spiritual leaders: one from the West and one from the East. Both talk about spirituality in a vague way. Neither make any radical truth claims but try to be open to everything. But how does that jibe with the real world, which is full of principles and laws and very real structure? *Wait a minute*, you might be saying. *It sounds like you are about to try to push organized religion on me. You can't do that because...*

- There's no proof God exists.
- There's no proof the resurrection of Christ took place.
- There's no proof believing in Jesus has positive value for a person.

Well, that's exactly what I thought. But I knew that there were millions of people in organized religion, so there had to be some kind of empirical evidence to garner such followings.

I have several friends who say entry into heaven requires a spiritual foundation, but not a specific ideology or doctrine. Often their spirituality is a mix of the major religions, sort of a buffet for what fits their palate. One of my agnostic friends says he's a spiritual person. He says his spirituality doesn't have a formal doctrine and doesn't have specific rules or criteria. "That's the great unknown," he says. "I don't think anyone really knows the rules. They act like they do, but they don't." For him there are no prophets, no specific leaders—not the Dalai Lama—and no governing body to decide guidelines.

I asked my friend if he had a place to go where he could meet with like-minded spiritual people and meditate or discuss their spirituality. Where would I go to find such spiritual people and maybe learn more about their version of spirituality? My friend said he isn't aware of a place for participants to meet since there isn't any doctrine or specific criteria. Sure, there may be a small contingent of members at a universal zen spiritual center, but those are usually only in large cities. But is there agreed-upon doctrine? If "doctrine" sounds too formal, are there principles that are universally consistent and used as the foundation of Spirituality with a capital S?

For some, *spirituality* may sound liberating and free. An equally strong argument could conclude the thesis is a house of cards. There's no formal structure for any level of measure. The doctrine would read something like this: "Each person does the best they can with criteria that can't be measured, nor does each person have or know any criteria or benchmarks. There are no current or past leaders. Each person makes up what works for them." When I recited this back to my friend, he said, "That's just it. If there were a detailed number for anything good or bad, God would spell it out, right? That's why I think he judges based on *individual criteria*."

It seemed like a circular argument to me: "I will be judged on criteria I don't know, and I'll do my best at criteria I don't know." The logic doesn't make sense to me, and it further breaks down when another person defines their idea of good, which you might think is bad. Likewise, it didn't make sense to me that you could have major religions contradicting each other. I had to find out what was the final authority that provides our measure.

I just couldn't rest in the idea of trying to live by an arbitrary concept of spirituality. I knew I had to wrestle with the Quran, Torah, Bible, and Vedas and be rigorous in my pursuit of one truth or 7.6 billion truths.

Questions:

1. If you say you're a spiritual but not religious person, are you essentially creating your own religion and hoping God agrees with you?

2. Is there a non-religious book that serves as *the* definitive spiritual book for people who choose spirituality as their faith or worldview?
3. If there is a heaven and hell, would you bet your eternal life on your personal definition of spirituality?

10

ALTERNATIVE SPIRITUALITY

"Alexander, Caesar, Charlemagne, and I have founded empires. But on what did we rest the creations of our genius? Upon force. Jesus Christ founded his empire upon love; and at this hour millions of men would die for him."

—Napoleon Bonaparte

One reason the idea of a vague spirituality was attractive to me was because I saw American Christianity as some jacked-up organization full of people trying to be perfect, "Why no, I haven't farted in almost three years." Yet they appeared incredibly hypocritical. Amen to that, us Christians are raging hypocrites, and I'm the poster child.

I'm a huge Johnny Cash fan. I knew he wasn't perfect, but he became a Christian. And he was the complete opposite of perfect, fart-free people—who don't exist anyway.

Johnny Cash had plenty of demons to battle, and he did so in raw, poignant songs. He painted a picture of God as a helper for the broken people of the world, which, lo and behold, happens to be all of us. I can relate to his fight: the desire to do right or fix myself, but the inability to be consistent with either. He seemed so genuine, clawing away each day while recognizing help is needed. In an article from *The Bitter Southerner* online newsletter in 2018, John Hayes writes about Cash's 1994 release *American Recordings*:

> And in the religious songs — more successfully woven into the artistic whole than on any Cash album before — salvation didn't belong to the upright and pious. It was for the broken-down and bereft, who achieved it through loneliness and lament.[1]

This is why I find Cash and U2's Bono spiritually attractive. They're rebels, for one. Bono impacts the world while also being a self-deprecating, f-bomb-dropping Irishman who has lifted a pint or three. Likewise, Cash didn't have patience for bullshit. Men like Bono and Cash strive to strip it away to get to the raw wound, then roll around in the stank.

When I'd hear the words *born again* or *evangelical*, I would groan. The same feeling with the word *sinner*. I thought the words sounded silly and certainly not cool. I preferred the word *mistake* in place of sin. *Mistake* is a word I could grasp. After looking at the other major religions, I kept coming back to this idea that Jesus Christ died for all of my past, present, and future *mistakes* and did the same for all of mankind. He did this at zero cost to me; it's a free gift for me to accept, or choose to take a pass. I think this message has gotten lost in all the religious dogma or right-wing conservatism. I thought being a Christian meant you automatically vote Republican, hate gay people, and generally see all those who are not Republicans and homophobic as evil leftists working as Satan's minions. But from my discovery, it seemed that Christianity starts with the unbelievably simple idea of deciding whether you want Jesus's free gift of forgiveness for your mistakes. It would be like someone offering me a free lunch every day for the rest of my life, with no strings attached, with no upfront commitment other than saying yes to accepting the free lunch... This couldn't be real.

As I explored, I realized what Jesus was saying was that every agnostic, atheist, Hindu, Buddhist, Muslim, and Jew will have to decide whether Christ died for them. If they disagree, they have to ask, does their religion or list of good deeds show more *good* than Christ? Meaning, when a devout Hindu, Buddhist, Muslim, or Jew says, "I pray, I go to temple or mosque, I try to love my neighbor and all my family and friends as best I can," does that outweigh the immeasurable love of someone dying on a cross for everyone's mistakes? (Remember those twelve trillion mistakes from chapter 7!)

But these other religions are Abrahamic, I thought. *They have historical veracity. How can they fall short?* I kept coming back to the idea that if the God of the Bible is true and real, his response will be the same question. God will say, "I sacrificed my Son for you and all people and all Muslims and all Jews. Does yours or any religion express a greater love than that?" This was hard to wrap my head around. I know there was no factual way all three religions could be right. In other words, why would God essentially trick people for whom he cares? Yes, the idea that God would give us three, or even three thousand, contradictory paths to know him would be the ruse of a madman. He would be a charlatan of the highest order using his power as a cosmic swindle.

In my search I came across a *Huffington Post* article on Buddhism.

> While the Buddha did discuss some metaphysical aspects of reality that people would often associate with religion, he made it clear that the most important aspect of Buddhism is how you practice, not what you know. A good example can be seen from the Cula-Malunkyovada Sutta, where the monk Venerable Malunkyaputta asks the Buddha a series of metaphysical questions such as whether: "The cosmos is eternal,' 'The cosmos is not eternal,' 'The cosmos is finite,' 'The cosmos is infinite,' 'The soul and the body are the same,' 'The soul is one thing and the body another..."[2]

> The Buddha responds to these inquiries by saying that such questions are not important and that asking such is like being shot by a poison arrow and saying, *"I won't have this arrow removed until I know the*

given name and clan name of the man who wounded me."
Of course, the logical thing to do would be to go
to a doctor about the wound rather than wasting
precious time asking such questions. So the lesson
is, knowing such things doesn't really have a use
and it's a waste of time to focus on them, that time
could be much better spent developing oneself.[3]

THIS is exactly why I needed to explore! The Buddha was
saying to focus on yourself and don't question whether the
cosmos is a God, whether it or he is eternal, and whether
my physical body is more than flesh, blood, and cells.

The Buddha assumed he was the final authority on
such matters. However, what if the cosmos (God) *IS* eternal, *IS* infinite, and *DOES* care about my soul? Here's the
key point to wrestle with: Buddha never claimed to be
God, never claimed deity. Christ did. Right there we have
to consider who has final authority between the two. One
says don't sweat eternity, one says it's very important and
HE is the key to the consideration.

Questions:

1. Does it help you to know that Christianity is
   designed for imperfect people?
2. If it turned out there are millions of people who
   are genuine, transparent, and possibly even cool
   like Johnny Cash and Bono, would Christianity be
   more attractive?

11

FIRE ANTS AND THE LAWNMOWER

"It suddenly struck me that that tiny pea, pretty and blue, was the Earth. I put up my thumb and shut one eye, and my thumb blotted out the planet Earth. I didn't feel like a giant. I felt very, very small."

—Neil Armstrong

One of the challenges we face as creatures with no supernatural powers other than navel-gazing is the perspective to understand the grand scheme of eternity. We have strong intellects; some minds are astounding, and we do our best to discern circumstances of what's happening in our individual lives. We turn on multiple channels of media to evaluate world events and do our best to educate ourselves, gain experience, and impart wisdom to our children. But life is unpredictable and tough, even in America where we experience affluence like few others. There's no shortage of tragedies and chaos that wear us down year after year and make us doubt there is any real meaning on the chessboard. Is there a God, let alone a God who cares? This can lead to apathy and cynicism about whether eternity exists. Should we spend precious moments in consideration in comparison to work, family, and a hundred other action items for the week? Our pride—or anxiety—then steps in and says, "I have to look out for number one," and FOMO and YOLO rule the day.

In the Old Testament of the Bible, I read a book called Proverbs. It's filled with wonderful little nuggets of wisdom such as Proverbs 16:18 (NIV): "Pride goes before destruction, a haughty spirit before a fall." The phrase "pride comes before the fall" is derived from this verse. There are a number of ways to see mankind's pride on display. Turn on the TV and watch experts in any field discussing their opinions on politics, sports, music, fashion, and food. Yes, many have earned their stripes and are genuine triumphs of knowledge. However, our selfie-obsessed social feeds show we're often overly exuberant about our lives. This adds to our blinders and numbs the desire to consider eternity, because we're caught up in our greatness in the moment.

This got me to thinking how small we may be in the grand scheme. As a young boy and all the way through high school, one of my chores was mowing the lawn. In Texas, cutting the grass also included obligatory wars against fire ants who had built their colonies in our yard. These ferocious little creatures would erect small piles of dirt throughout the yard. If you've watched insect documentaries, you know how robust these entities can be. Ant colonies range in size from several hundred workers per queen to several million with trails leading to other colonies. Think of them as small cities.

As I cut the grass with our lawnmower, I would run over the "ant beds." The top portion of their colony would shoot out the side of the lawnmower, and the colony would react as if WWIII had erupted. In their eyes, a great mechanized beast had rolled into their domain with fearsome, weaponized blades and a deafening noise that rumbled their city to smithereens. I would often stop to watch the chaos I created as thousands of ants scrambled to destroy the intruder. Many times, I inadvertently stepped into this frenzied melee, and the angry ants would wreak havoc on my legs with their stings.

To these warring ants, it was the equivalent of an earthquake devastating their city. Little did they know the disturbance was not a natural disaster or war, it was simply some schmoe cutting his grass on a Sunday afternoon on his day off from work. And this same schmoe was one of 7.6 billion others in a larger menagerie of cities.

The ants have a limited perspective. From their point of view, an evil invader has purposely ruined their home. A war had started, and they must fight to survive! The same goes for us. A spouse comes home and asks for a divorce. A car accident takes the life of a loved one. A natural disaster disrupts life as we know it, and it takes years if not decades to recover. Are we no different than the ants? From our limited perspective, we don't have the capacity to understand how the chess pieces are being moved. We respond with the same anger and fervor as the ants when one moment life was humming along, and the next our world explodes. I scratch my head with confusion or shake my fist while screaming f-bombs when I see the terrible things taking place in our world. However, what if it turns out all those disruptions in our life are part of a larger plan being played out? I thought about what if, in the midst of perceived chaos, there were a benevolent God who will explain every last detail when we arrive in heaven? I struggled to believe there is a heaven where a God who cares exists. It's the human condition to view disruptions in our lives with the same ferocity as the ants. But what if, just *MAYBE*, the epic catastrophes in our lives turn out to be the equivalent of losing a sock in the dryer, when we'll be living in a perfect heaven for all of time. Can I grasp that and hold the tension? Some days it's impossible in the midst of the pain and disappointment. The tsunamis of life can level us like Mike Tyson in his prime. However, the gap between the ants understanding what I did as a twelve-year-old kid mowing the lawn, seems similar to the gap in our efforts to comprehend every cosmic maneuver from God. To steal a great line from a pastor friend: It's like trying to explain television to a dog.

Questions:

1. Have you struggled with believing in a God who loves you, due to tragedies that have devastated your life?
2. Is it possible for you to take a step and trust God when circumstances say otherwise? Could there be a larger narrative being played out that might be explained at a later time?
3. Do people often have too much hubris in thinking they deserve an explanation from the being who created them?

12

THE UPSIDE-DOWN PYRAMID

"Fear never scaled one mountain, never stepped up on a stage, never accepted a challenge, never tilled new ground, never walked in a race; he never even dared to dream. Fear failed to slay a single dragon. Remember this before you choose to keep his company."

—Richelle E. Goodrich, *Slaying Dragons*

I didn't grow up in a religious household, and if we went to church, it was only on Easter and Christmas. We didn't pray before meals, and God was never mentioned or discussed in any capacity. In hindsight I wouldn't say we were atheistic or antagonistic towards God; he just wasn't part of the program.

As I became an adult, if the topic of Christianity was discussed, I smugly thought those people were weak and looking for a crutch in life. I assumed I didn't need it. Plus, I thought if I did become a Christian, I would be required to listen to Amy Grant and wear Dockers dress pants. (Are those still around?) Apologies to Amy Grant and wearers of Dockers, but we're all entitled to subjective tastes. I assumed I would change and become a straitlaced shadow of myself. I didn't think I would be able to enjoy a good beer and cigar and could no longer listen to Jane's Addiction, Tom Waits, and the Pixies.

I had a view of faith in Christ as a pyramid. As the three edges of the pyramid go upward, they continue narrowing into a point. In my mind, Christianity would shatter my current life, which seemed to be wide open, and narrow it to a small point as I got closer to God. I thought of it as constrictive, hemming people into a boring funnel. As I considered death and what it meant to be good enough, and as I explored other religions, I came back to this Christianity. I started to see how putting your faith in Jesus Christ inverts the pyramid. I didn't realize how deficient my current life was, dancing on a tiny tip of a pyramid. As I believed more deeply and grew in my understanding of Christ, my life widened and became impactful, with richer, deeper perception. I became more woke, with increased interest in varied topics; everything had a new lens for viewing. I found my creativity heightened, and since that's how I make my living, I naturally wanted to tap into the spigot. The evidence of the inversion of the pyramid is the stunning experiences I've had via humanitarian aid trips around the world, the people I've met stateside and abroad, and the thought-provoking doors that opened from pursuing my faith.

I categorize this pyramid idea as a fear of losing oneself. I understand. But what if following Christ makes you more like your rebellious heroes, as opposed to SNL's Dana Carvey playing the Church Lady? We all want to be the best or truest version of ourselves. Any change for the better often requires choices and effort that causes discomfort or the possibility of pain. At the very least, there's an obstinance in us, stemming from fear of the unknown. Even when we know the change will be for our benefit, an inertia exists in taking those steps, primarily due to a perceived loss of control. This is true. When opening up to the idea of believing in God and possibly having an actual relationship with him, we relinquish control as we move closer to believing and following his movements in our lives. However, it's comforting to realize that by pursuing God, I will become the best version of me. In fact, it's the only chance I have of achieving my truest self. If not, I fall back to the traditional pyramid concept: I become smaller and less impactful. I don't want to risk the chance.

Writer Melissa Gilbert in her fantastic 2009 TED Talk "The Elusive Creative Genius" mentions creativity possibly coming from a mysterious outside force. In her talk, there's an awe and wonder as to where the creative spark is derived. She tiptoes right up to the edge of discussing God as the possible origin, but then gently saunters away. She concludes by saying it's presumptuous to assume we humans are able to generate the magic on our own. I agree with the latter viewpoint. Regarding God as the spark, for all of us, maybe there's trepidation; it's simply too big of a leap to question whether God is channeling the creative juice through us as conduits.

However, we often hear references to deity being the source of inspiration. As a guitar geek, I've heard several musicians refer to Jimi Hendrix as a conduit for God's music flowing through him; the guitar was simply an extension of his heart and body. It seems reasonable that Jimi himself, or Melissa Gilbert, or any artist is simply an extension of God's creativity. Let's take it a step further and ask if the creativity is God operating through his son, Jesus Christ?

This is where the rub begins. As mentioned above, before I believed in Christ, I was okay with the idea of God painting through me or working through me. But all the man-made baggage with Christianity made me shun the idea. Would I have to vote Republican on all issues? I can't hang out with my gay friends! Egads, Christianity will make me boring! Will I no longer have any fun?

These fears were vanquished when I realized the overwhelming love generated from seeking Christ… as God… were one and the same. Now the upside-down pyramid continues to expand upwards, generating a larger life and boundless worldview.

Questions:

1. What anxiety or fear do you have in thinking of Christ as the missing piece in your life?

2. What fears do you have in relation to the pyramid narrowing towards God? Are you worried you'll be hypnotized into becoming a shell of yourself? Concerned you'll have to give up fun?

13

THE WATCH BUILDS ITSELF

*"For a thing's beauty we ought to compliment not
its owner, but its maker."*

—Mokokoma Mokhonoana

One of the aspects of my world that expanded when I started to believe in Christ was what I thought about evolution and intelligent design. I remember vehemently disagreeing with the creationist thesis. I could never get past the famous illustration of the ape slowly morphing from a hunched-over, knuckle-dragging primate to an upright, standing man. I can hear myself saying, "Come on, only a moron would disagree with the evolutionary model." This issue was a major hurdle for me before I became a hypnotized puppet of Christ, drinking the poisonous Kool-Aid in the Bible belt. (Bam, a little sarcasm. I love to poke fun at us Jesus freaks.) Then that pesky God fella stepped in and took my knees out. If there were an Ultimate Boss with a capital U and a capital B, there had to be a Creator. How to navigate evolution was an epiphany for me, and hopefully my stab at the discussion helps you view the prism with new eyes.

As an artist I'm diligent in how I combine colors to create vibrancy with light. Or when I use cooler temperament colors to create shadows. Often I have to take a break from the canvas and watch various documentaries to relax. Many show an underwater sea world teeming with diversity. The colors are spellbinding, and I try to imagine the challenge of matching those colors. It would require twenty years of intense training for me to be able to piece together the tapestry of one small scene from the ocean and translate the spectrum on to a canvas. The precision needed would tax every synapse of my right brain. There are millions upon millions of creatures, each species with unique patterns, each with unique instincts and brains.

Yet somehow I believed evolution created millions of patterns without any ability to evaluate light and shadow or to have a conception of how colors interact. In other words, evolution created creatures with a brain, while not having a brain. Yes, that would fall under things that make you go *hmm*, or, in my mind, what sounds like a Grand Canyon sized leap of faith.

Think of it like this. The technological revolution was a phase of rapid industrialization in the final third of the twentieth and twenty-first century. During this time, people engineered and created advanced technology in increasingly faster increments. Consider the capabilities of smart phones; they connect people from around the world and do so from the palms of our hands. All that enormous horsepower came from intelligent minds making choices and intricate plans for a desired outcome.

Yet the entities who created the spectacular technology, all with exact binary code and various disciplines of engineering, were supposed to be created by random chance. Really?

My world started opening up.

There are countless sleep-inducing videos on YouTube, and I'm not claiming expertise on the Socratic method of debate. The discussion between evolutionists and creationists centers around the idea of causation. In the Merriam-Webster dictionary, evolution is defined as "a process in which the whole universe is a progression of interrelated phenomena." Another definition says it's "a process of change in a certain direction." The Big Bang is today's dominant scientific conjecture about the origin of the universe.

Our universe was born about 13.7 billion years ago in a massive expansion that blew space up like a gigantic balloon. That, in a nutshell, is the Big Bang theory, which virtually all cosmologists and theoretical physicists endorse... A dominant idea that connects the dots between the Big Bang and the universe we find today is called inflation. This is the notion that during the first roughly 10 to the minus 34 seconds (0.000000000000000000000 000000000001 seconds), the universe underwent exponential expansion, doubling in size at least 90 times. During this early stage, matter was in a much different state than it is now... These newly created atoms were all positively charged, as the universe was still too hot to favor the capture of electrons. But that changed about 380,000 years after the Big Bang. In an epoch known as recombination, hydrogen and helium ions began snagging electrons, forming electrically neutral atoms. Light scatters significantly off free electrons and protons, but much less so off neutral atoms. So photons were now much more free to cruise through the universe... Over time, stars gravitated together to form galaxies, leading to more and more large-scale structure in the universe. Planets coalesced around some newly forming stars, including our own sun. And 3.8 billion years ago, life took root on Earth.[1]

In a nutshell, the basic premise of today's scientific worldview believes *EVERYTHING* we see today in this world is the result of a cosmic accident. Processes such as *ekpyrotic*, *inflation*, *recombination*, and *reionization* randomly occurred. Meaning that several billion years ago a *singular* event began expanding the universe. Then, with the addition of time, *millions and millions of years* as Carl Sagan often said, all things (nature, animals, people, dirt, water, air) came into being. Whether or not you buy into the Big Bang, the argument states evolution is part of this inflation and works independently as the origin of all things. A trigger, circumstance, or action occurred, and the evolution of all matter resulted in the world we see today. Regardless of how many scientific polysyllabic words you add to the discussion, the only variables are a cause-agent and time. And the cause agent *IS NOT* and *WAS NOT* God.

Many people think science is the answer to all of life's big questions. I *ALSO* thought science was the answer to all of life's big questions. And eventually science would understand all things once we've tested and analyzed enough items. But science has not always been a major discipline. The methodology of science was created by men. Science didn't simply happen; it's a thing we created as a mechanism for measurement and evaluation. It was not a generator of energy, or a thing-maker, for lack of a better description. For instance, Aristotle and Plato are thought to be the founders of empirical science. And they lived in the third century BC. There are numerous references to Hasan Ibn al-Haytham as the architect of the scientific method. He lived in the ninth century AD, which was the beginning of the golden age of Islam. The development of a scientific process similar to the modern method was then developed by Muslim scholars between the tenth and fourteenth centuries. Many historians regard this as the starting period of science.[3] Galileo has been called the "father of observational astronomy," the "father of modern physics," the "father of the scientific method,"[4] and even the "father of science."[5] He lived in the early 1600s. So clearly science was not a thing that existed at the beginning of time. And it has progressed or evolved through the ages. Even a description of Aristotle says, "His writings cover many subjects—including physics, biology, zoology, metaphysics, logic, ethics, aesthetics, poetry, theatre, music, rhetoric, psychology, linguistics, economics, politics and government."[6] Every item on the list is a created thing that came from structure and purpose. Yes, I recognize that science as a word is the nomenclature we apply to all the evolutionary processes. But my point is that we treat it like the master engineer instead of the study of the engineer's toys.

It's the methodology, not the mechanism. We want to view science as the thing behind the curtain creating the magic. We expect to pull back the covering to see the intricate beauty and complexity occurring, the processes generating energy and matter, and say, "Wow, look at that science!" Except science isn't the thing. It's more like one of many manuals explaining an entity a thousand times bigger than the bucket of science. We should say, "Damn, my tool of science has helped me see attributes of the most incredible artist who created and curated the entire universe. Amazing!"

In my journey I have discovered that creationism and evolution absolutely can coexist, but with an intelligent being who controls the mechanisms and paths. My explanation above is the dumbed-down version, but that is the debate.

An evolutionist cannot move outside the lane of using time and shit happening as the only variables in the equation. Even Merriam-Webster says there's a *process* that ties together the *interrelated phenomena,* which begins to unravel the evolutionist's thesis because those italicized words sound purposeful and designed. When you say something is a process, you beg the question: What was the cause—or reason or purpose or event—that drove the process, the next explosions, or the next singularity. Without some manner of purpose, none of the first actions or causation can occur, and certainly any events thereafter must have a cause. Even a survival-of-the-fittest thesis has time as the only mechanism to drive change. Any perceived change of direction or choice or strategy disproves the evolutionist thesis because choice, direction, and strategy require cognitive reason, which is the argument of the creationist camp. Here are three practical examples for comprehension of the intelligent design argument.

1) Look at a chess board. When you see red and black squares, you immediately discern a pattern. Patterns prove design, because there's no randomness. A game designer purposely created the squares as part of the game. Therefore, if one singular event occurred as the source of all creation, any major events, such as species jumping across DNA ladders, must be random for the thesis of evolution to maintain its truth. The singular events cannot form a pattern, because pattern implies

structure—like a checkerboard—which implies intelligence from design.

2) We've all seen the stunning symmetry of snow-flakes. Evolution alone could not form and main-tain such a detailed structure. The intricate design and balanced proportions couldn't happen at ran-dom. Evolution cannot *think* or *discern* symmetry, the mechanism doesn't exist to measure the vari-ables, or know how to consider what balance means. It's like a chef building a rack of unique spices with no comprehension of how taste buds function.

3) When I look at a house or building, I know an architect designed the foundation, the walls, and all the elements inside to form functional rooms. The building did not form itself based solely on time, *millions and millions of years*, and tah-dah, the structure came together with perfect form and function. Every building, every home, every street, every wheel, every designed thing came from intel-ligent planning. There's nothing random involved.

A more compelling discussion involves the idea of a watch, a riff on eighteenth century philosopher William Paley's position on natural theology. I can't recall where I first heard this, but it's not a thesis I developed. Let's say I had a Swiss watch and beat it into a thousand pieces with a ham-mer. I then took the pieces and placed them in a box and taped it shut. What if I built a machine that gently shook the box for 1,000 or 10,000 or 100,000 years? Does it seem feasible the watch would reform itself? The gut reaction is, "Of course not! Not in a million years!" Evolutionists claim that with enough time, the watch could reform, as would a house or a building. Whether one million or 100 million years, could those structures form themselves without a purposeful designer guiding the outcome? Is there a reasonable explanation? Or is there statistical significance to disprove the null hypothesis of "all life randomly created itself"?

The same goes for people. An evolutionist claims with enough time we've evolved into the complex organisms we see today, without any entity or God helping push the process. We started as ooze and randomly ended up as laughing, crying, depth-filled entities who can plan, create, love, have sex and orgasms, build complex machines and computers, and miraculously heal. We evolved into ourselves without any rhyme, reason, or foundation of direction. Nothing but ooze that just decided to move…. Wait, dammit, I used the word *decided*. How could ooze decide to forge a path? How could evolution fathom where to start the process of healing, let alone build the engine to propel the blood? Doubtful. More than likely, an intelligent agent began the process.

Maybe this brings it home for you. Whether you're with two friends, a group of twenty, or in an auditorium with 5,000, there's a high probability most people have two arms, two legs, two eyes, eight fingers and two thumbs. This is another example of a pattern. Now add in the complexities of generating life and thousands of unique species of lives. How could all this purposefully designed activity occur without a driver pulling the levers? And, no, any anomalies and deformities that occur don't break the idea of design; they're simply a one-off imperfection to the model.

Forgive me for sending you into a coma with this rabbit trail. Why does it matter? Intelligent design speaks to the existence of a boss, and whether we answer to said boss. An intelligent designer might very well be God; and he may be the doorman into an eternal paradise. This is a crucial point to wrestle with in the grand scheme of trying to be good eggs as a means to earn entrance into the never-never land of guilt-free sex, 24/7 rock and roll, and all-you-can-eat bacon and pancakes.

Questions:

1. When you make a decision, is it a procedure activated with utter randomness, or do you use your brain in the process? Think about the idea of selection and choice. Can evolution make any manner of calculation to improve or divert, and do it without intelligence?

2. If you could live for ten million years, and you stood and hovered over a pile of mud, would it eventually evolve into a spouse? Consider if there is reasonable evidence to think water, dirt, air, gases, and fire could form human life without guidance?

14

THE TOOTH-FAIRY, SANTA CLAUS, AND BIGFOOT

"Seeing is not believing, it is only seeing."

—George MacDonald, *The Princess and the Goblin*

As an eight-year-old boy, like many kiddos I would leave a cookie on the fireplace mantel the night before Christmas. The next morning I'd race downstairs to see all my loot from the great bearded fellow who came and went via the chimney. Such an astoundingly crisp dude he was, delivering those toys all over the world, like FedEx on 'roids. I for sure knew my cookie helped fuel his marathon, because I could see the evidence… a single bite mark in the cookie and a half-empty glass of milk.

Somewhere around the age of nine, ten, or eleven, the bubble burst and I realized the mirage of Santa was actually my mom and pop playing the role. They were quite talented and generous in characterizing good Saint Nick, and I was blessed big-time. On a smaller scale and around the same age, I also came to realize there wasn't a bunny crappin' out candy every year on Easter; nor was there a racketeering fairy who bootlegged children's teeth as contraband for a few bucks under my pillow. This awareness caused little anxiety, and I stepped into the next years of life without a scar.

During my teens, I became fascinated with Bigfoot. Simply reading the name may bring to mind grainy images of a hairy figure that looks like a guy in a gorilla suit. Remember the grainy 8mm film of him disappearing into the woods? Damn, I wanted that film to be proof of his existence.

Fast-forward another ten years, and the idea of religion and Jesus Christ would occasionally come across my path. Maybe an acquaintance would mention it in passing. More dramatically, when I was twenty-two a dear friend who had a complete life turnaround sat with me to discuss the lever that changed him. We had been classmates in high school, but he and I ran in different circles. I remember he smoked a lot of weed, and I was the typical meathead jock playing basketball. Somehow we both ended up in honors math and English classes, meatheadedness and weed notwithstanding.

Years later I saw him a few months before college graduation, and he was *COMPLETELY* different. He was toned, tan, and had a glow about him. I asked him what had happened that gave him the aura emanating from his eyes. He responded that he had bottomed out on meth and had been robbing food out of the back of grocery stores with his brother. He had flirted with the wrong side of the law and recognized in the fog of meth highs that his life was sinking. During one of the darkest nights, he fell face down on his bed and pleaded for God to help him—and shazam, he did. He surrendered his life to Christ, and over the next three months cleaned up his act. He had a couple of lapses, I remember him saying in answer to my skepticism, but, no bones about it, his 180-turn was due to Christ working in his life. Through teary eyes, he asked if I would like to know Christ as he did. I remember saying, "Good for you, brother, but not for me."

At the time, and for the next ten years, if I did think about religion, the only time of day I had the thought was, "Why keep believing in Santa Claus as an adult?" I mean, aren't we supposed to move past childish fantasies of fairies, bunnies, and a jolly red-suited man? By the age of twelve, only the rarest of kids still believe in those gift-giving entities. Or in the case of Bigfoot, a small fringe element holds on to the idea of a half-ape, half-man stalking the redwood forest. Wouldn't the same hold true for a two-thousand-year-old myth? At some point, wouldn't men and women in maybe the year AD 300 have said, "Come on folks, this Christ stuff died out years ago! Time to move on to real life!"

I had thought it was a waste of time to believe in God. Bestselling authors Richard Dawkins and Sam Harris argue that if religious people would simply let go of their silly superstitions, mankind could move on to a more intellectually focused culture with science as the chauffeur. However, years later I started to see my friend's story through a different lens. I began to realize that I've yet to hear anyone say they discovered atheism and it changed their life, in the same way a person experiences the grace of Christ. As I perused some of the hundreds of videos at the testimonial website *IAmSecond.com* and heard people from all walks of life pointing to Jesus Christ as their impetus for change, I couldn't help but wonder why there isn't a similar site full of hundreds of atheists claiming great life changes due to their non-belief in God.

I wondered if maybe the hundreds of people on *IAmSecond.com* were delusional and had somehow wrongly assumed Christ affected them. But in actuality, it was something else, an unknowable scientific process that fired from the synapses in their brains. Those chemicals must've altered their thinking and turned them into wish-based zombies. I've also met incarcerated men who *unequivocally* say prison is the best thing that ever happened to them because they met Jesus Christ while locked up. Uh, whuh? I guess they're zombies, too. As are another 500,000 people you could search for online who've had similar experiences. Pure irrationality. Which means the other 2.1 billion strong who have laid claim to this God-esque Easter bunny as the driving force of their lives are complete whack-jobs.

If it were all some hoax, I thought, wouldn't the superstition have ended centuries ago? As mentioned, I've outgrown Santa Claus and the tooth fairy; I discovered their true identities by the age of ten.

Stripping away everything I said in the previous chapter about empirical evidence of design, if atheists had discovered the cure for the ill of religious superstition, wouldn't the hunger for the pill be ravenous? The longing for a spiritual cure would cease, and people would no longer claim life-change based on connecting with God. If atheism is true, our highly intelligent brains would put away childish things, right? It seems 80 to 90 percent of the world who believe in a deity would come to their senses by the age of fifteen, and certainly by the age of thirty. I mean, do you know any twenty-year-old people still waking up at 3:00 a.m. in their jammies to leave a cookie on the fireplace?

Yet millions of people around the world every year claim faith in an intelligent designer in the form of Jesus Christ. This made me pause. I was further on my journey. I figured maybe life was more than just the here and now with me driving the car of life.

Questions

1. If you've met someone who claims their life changed when they declared faith in Jesus Christ, are there any plausible explanations other than it being true? Discuss your reasons with them.

2. Are there other superstitions you know of that have lasted for centuries? Are there institutions around the world devoted to studying them? Are there credible academics and laypeople who all point to these superstitions as the most important component of their lives?

15

WHO'S THE REAL BOSS?

"When his life was ruined, his family killed, his farm destroyed, Job knelt down on the ground and yelled up to the heavens, 'Why god? Why me?' and the thundering voice of God answered, There's just something about you that pisses me off."

—Stephen King, *Storm of the Century*

Please, can we all focus all energies on my navel? By far, the most important goal in life is for you to realize how your life relates to mine. My family, friends, and strangers are in dire need of this life lesson. Yes, I care about you… in relation to me.

Oh, if only I were being facetious. If I'm a measure of the multitudes, then we spend tremendous amounts of time thinking of all things… in relation to us being the center of the known universe. It's difficult to fully comprehend how much we focus on self. Take a moment and consider your spouse, kids, work, anything that comes to mind. All circumstances pretty much revolve around the impact on *ME*. It's astonishing when I think of something that's other-focused, like praying for friends; I quickly evaluate how much time it will take. Will they approve? Will they appreciate the gesture? Fascinating… and I'm referring to prayer, which by definition should be tinged with humility. Our inherent selfishness impacts our perception of being told what to do, no matter how effective the messenger, particularly if the message comes from a stereotype of the proverbial boss.

At our most basic existence, we are accustomed to the idea of *authority*. The word may make us buck. Maybe it sounds domineering or rigid. Nonetheless, authority provides order in our lives. A two-year-old knows their parents are the heads of state. For the child, there is automatic recognition of this fact. As the child grows, they're introduced to teachers who are understood to be authorities. Then maybe coaches come into the picture, along with other instructors, maybe a ballet or music instructor. When we become teenagers, a crucial benchmark in life occurs when we get our first job and have a boss. Regardless of whether the first boss may be an eighteen-year-old with acne and a voice still cracking, many of us experience having a boss while we're still teenagers, not yet old enough to be adults. By the time we're in our early twenties, 99 percent of people have a boss who provides directives for work. Entrepreneurs who start and run companies ultimately answer to consumers who control via purchasing power whether their company continues or not. If we look at the military, the entire structure is based on a hierarchy of top-down or bottom-up authority. A private has a corporal, and submission to your superior officer is absolute. At each rank there's another rank who is a superior. At the highest ranks there's a colonel and ultimately a general. Among those generals, there's one-star, two-star, three-star, and four-star generals. Even the mafia mirrors military hierarchy, with families having capos and crews who serve as a form of platoons to serve the family business, albeit unlawfully.

I mention these examples to show how accustomed we are to authority in our lives. The question is: how much authority do we have? As in, are you the ultimate boss? For our discussion, let's consider how authoritative your opinion is. In our postmodern culture, we've adopted the posture that our opinions can supersede facts and truth. I wholeheartedly think a person's opinion has value, and every person should find their voice for what they stand for and believe. But an opinion does not override truth, and it seems unlikely if not outrageous that my little ol' opinion would carry more weight than God's.

Let's look at practical examples of authority. In the world in which we live, do we set the tone and leave things ambiguous without measure? No. For example, does an NBA player show up with his own definition of an NBA game and play however he feels, running without dribbling, declaring when he scores a basket that it counts for seven points instead of two or three? Does the NBA say, "Sure, whatever works for you?" No, he follows accepted rules and guidelines, which showcase his talent, and other players use the same standards. This creates a level playing field to evaluate the individual players and allows the game to flourish without ambiguity. Imagine if the player showed up to the NBA finals with no practice, no idea of how the game was played, no way of knowing how the score was kept… and then hoped he didn't lose. Imagine if every player did the same; there would be no way to evaluate wins or losses, there would be no semblance of an actual game. Pick any sport; the athletes don't simply "try their best." To measure good, great, average, or bad, there are scores. Why do we know LeBron James and Kareem Abdul-Jabbar are great basketball players, and not just decent? We look at scoring averages and number of All-Star appearances and NBA Championships. We compare them to other NBA greats throughout the history of basketball; and look to the NBA's history as final authority.

Here's another real-world example. I don't have the right to walk into the office of the CEO of the company I work for and say, "Look, chief, this is how I roll. You just deal with it and accept my authority." Can I walk into my annual performance review and tell my boss, "The sales quota doesn't matter, I simply did my best, and that should be enough?" In other words, would you sign a contract and agree to work for a company that had no performance reviews in writing, never explained how you get a raise, and never explained how you get fired? It's like creating a company with no formal incorporation or standards. The company couldn't survive or begin in the first place. In our work lives we're accustomed to accepting policies and procedures from a higher authority or board of directors who have established guidelines, benchmarks, and procedures for us to follow.

Maybe this track sounds narrow and rigid. Let's look at the arts. The most creative musician or painter is working within accepted boundaries of their instrument and medium. A guitarist uses proven and absolute scales that create notes and melodies. They don't insist on playing totally free and random notes to create a song. The sound would be disjointed and break the rules of music (Coltrane and Monk fans notwithstanding, they still had melodic foundations). A writer can't simply type random letters of the alphabet and call them words and language. Structure and calculated rhythm form sentences and a narrative. I have another career as a visual artist. I follow principles of color, light, and shadow. Plus, does the canvas tell me how to paint? No, I'm the creator, so I set the guidelines for the paint being applied to the canvas. The created thing doesn't dictate to the creator, particularly if it's Creator with a capital C. Again, this alludes to who's the final boss of our lives. Even if you said a painter is allowed absolute freedom to use paint however he or she pleases, there is a point where the paint no longer is viewed as pleasurable, it's simply "mud" on the canvas and no longer art. The same applies to music. Yes, a musician is absolutely free to hit every note on every fret, but this is not the definition of scales or music, it's simply noise from an instrument that is being played wrong.

Errrrrrrt! I hear the needle scratching the record. Please don't jet just yet. In my experience, plenty of folks call bullshit on the idea of God because he appears to be an evil baddie whose sole purpose is the destruction of our lives. I hear ya; there are plenty of days I hop off the bus due to the hundredth crap story of the week. Man, I get it. This colors everything about this book. Do I truly believe what I'm writing, and how I'm connecting the dots to life after death? Often I have to grab the life preserver and play back all the times I know God was real, and I question whether I'm lucid or delusional. And, yes, most importantly, I question his love.

At the core of the exercise or argument about being *good* and *good enough* for the next life is a question of who's in charge. I'm referring to who's in charge of the world and universe we occupy.

Many people say they don't believe in organized religion. When pressed to define what that means, friends say, "I'm a spiritual person, and I don't believe something MAN-made." By this they're referring to religious texts authored by men and women. If a person says they dismiss religious texts, and instead prefer a list or personal moral code they live by, they believe they are the ultimate authority. How so? Because they've determined if there is a God, then he, she, or it will submit to their personal definition. Remember, in this example the person has removed belief in man-made religious texts. They're saying the creator now submits to them, the created thing. If the person says, "No, I still think God is in charge, but I'll be judged according to how I lived my life," they've validated my point: we think *WE'RE* in charge and God answers to us. Keep in mind, any definition or list or document authored by a person is also man-made.

Maybe you're scratching your head right about now. We all live by laws and rules in every facet of life. In the United States, we have a written constitution with a Supreme Court of judges who assess whether U.S. citizens are accurately abiding by the laws in the constitution.

Therefore, does it sound plausible that the creator of the universe would likely be the ultimate boss? Meaning, wouldn't this boss have an opinion about the things he created? In other words, would the boss let the employees tell him or her how to run the company? Not likely on this side of eternity. So why would the concept change when measuring how to enter heaven?

One common idea is the concept of God as timekeeper. He created all things, but then stepped back with folded arms and now takes a passive position, with his only role as a timekeeper. In this concept, God isn't a referee who calls the game with balls and strikes or foul balls. He lets the clock tick and watches world events and people navigate circumstances without interference. This idea has challenges because we regularly hear people say they witnessed a miracle, whether someone cured of an illness or having walked away from a car wreck. Or, if you're a Chicago Cubs fan, winning the World Series in 2015 (apologies to

Chicagoans!). In other words, some circumstances and outcomes do appear to say there is an active God who does intervene at times. One reason we see God as a passive timekeeper is the presence of tragedy, particularly if it comes in the form of evil. We have limited perception of the entire tapestry, therefore we make a broad generalization that God is not engaged when evil occurs.

For example, I recently watched an excellent series on ESPN called "Basketball: A Love Story." There was a compelling story of a hall of fame player named Maurice Stokes. He played for the Cincinnati Royals from 1955 to 1958. At the age of twenty-five, when his career was taking off, he suffered a head injury during a game, which led to complete paralysis. Although permanently paralyzed, Stokes was mentally alert and communicated by blinking his eyes. He adopted a grueling physical therapy regimen that eventually allowed him limited physical movement. He spent three years typing his own autobiography, which was never published.[1]

While watching this segment on Stokes play out, I could feel my frustration growing with the boss, as in God. I was shaking my head, as doubt set in regarding my own struggles in believing God is more than a timekeeper. "Do you really care about us?" I thought. As the story continued, the narrative mentioned that during the years that followed, Stokes was supported and cared for by his lifelong friend and teammate, Jack Twyman, who became Stokes's legal guardian. Twyman organized a charity exhibition basketball game in 1958 to help raise funds for Stokes's medical expenses. The event became an annual tradition and was named the Maurice Stokes Memorial Basketball Game. The episode fast-forwarded to Twyman speaking at the hall of fame ceremony when Stokes was inducted. Twyman mentioned, "by the grace of God I was able to know Maurice Stokes." The documentary then segued into how this event with Stokes led to players realizing how little protection they had in terms of insurance and pensions if a devastating injury occurred. This led to a threatened boycott of an NBA All-Star game, which ultimately led to the NBA establishing a pension plan for NBA players.

What came to mind was the idea that in the midst of perceived tragedy, maybe God—the boss—was not simply a timekeeper. Maybe he was working in Twyman's heart and in others' to move the chess pieces, which ultimately resulted in a successful outcome with NBA players receiving pensions. Does my opinion, if accurate, completely reconcile the tragedy of Maurice Stokes life? Tough to say. Judging by the Twyman family's insight, I would assume yes: the good outweighed the bad. You might also think the family's opinion in no way proves God had anything to do with the events and outcome. I agree. But it at least provides an alternative to the concept of God as only a passive timekeeper.

I'm not here to debate the merit or feasibility of miracles, nor is this a book focused on why God does or doesn't intervene. That's a challenge for the greatest of minds, and way above my paygrade—all our paygrades, in my opinion. What I am saying is a detailed creator would seem to prefer active engagement with his creation, the same as a parent raising a child. The timekeeper concept seems illogical when the complex details of this world are considered.

Maybe the word *boss* connotes a vision of a controlling ogre. Possibly he is. But, if we look at the wonderful elements we see in nature, or the feeling of falling in love, or an outcome such as Maurice Stokes, maybe this ultimate boss is benevolent and caring. It certainly seems plausible to assume God might care about his creation. Tragic accidents and horrific deaths cause us to doubt the goodwill of God, but there may be an explanation for the bad things we see and experience personally and witness on a global level. Again, the explanation might not placate us on this side of heaven, but maybe in the next life we'll be able to reconcile tragedies.

If someone uses the analogy of presenting a case to God the judge, the plaintiff is measured against existing laws in place. In other words, God judges according to established rules he's framed. The created thing—us—doesn't dictate back to the creator—God. Even secular philosophers agree that the created thing doesn't dictate to the creator. The more powerful entity sets the standards for lesser beings. God is the boss, not us. We don't always like our boss on this side of heaven, and we may not agree with everything God the boss says. But God is the boss.

Here's the other side of the argument regarding who's the boss. If a person believes in the Quran, Torah, or Bible, they believe God is in charge. Yes, all religious texts are man-made, but all the authors in those books subjugate themselves to a higher authority who is dictating the point of view. This posture is a substantial—and humble—difference. Even a casual read through the Old and New Testaments of the Bible will show how all the authors have an inherent modesty and reverential awe toward the Lord, who has included them in the dialogue as vessels and conduits for his message. Amazing!

Do you see the overall problem? We want to be the final authority in our own lives. The problem is, we're not God. It sounds crazy to have to write it out, but, as mentioned, our pride and hubris are spectacular at times. Everything would be fine if we set the standard, but we don't.

But let's close this chapter with the image of a benevolent manager, someone who cares about you as a person a thousand times more than the bottom line of revenue and profits. Combine Jimmy Stewart from *It's a Wonderful Life*, Santa Claus, and as many warm and fuzzy characters as you can imagine—that's the leader we want to know.

Questions:

1. When you think of a boss, are there positive or negative reactions?
2. Do you see people as the sole individual boss of their lives, or do they answer to a higher authority?

16

ALL RELIGIONS ARE THE SAME

"Religion has actually convinced people that there's an invisible man living in the sky who watches everything you do, every minute of every day. And the invisible man has a special list of ten things he does not want you to do. And if you do any of these ten things, he has a special place, full of fire and smoke and burning and torture and anguish, where he will send you to live and suffer and burn and choke and scream and cry forever and ever 'til the end of time! But He loves you. He loves you, and He needs money! He always needs money! He's all-powerful, all-perfect, all-knowing, and all-wise, somehow just can't handle money!"

—George Carlin

There's a common belief that like ice cream, religions are essentially different flavors of milk and sugar—some prefer strawberry or fundamentalist vanilla—and if you want something eclectic, pick Häagen-Dazs® coconut macaroon. We have seen how we are accustomed to guidelines in our lives. We have rules for all sorts of things from driving to sports to music and art. When discussing world religions, it seems logical to think religions are no different. In the UK, people drive on the left side of the road compared to the USA. However, while the specifics of speed limits and which side of the road to drive on might be different, all drivers are following the country's rules when driving in order to keep some sense of order. Religion seems similar in that if you picture God at the top of a mountain, you may think there are multiple ways to ascend to him, but each road has a slightly different set of rules, such as different speed limits and different sides of the road to drive on. We like to take a bottom-up approach and hope as long as we choose a path going up, we're fine. This analogy works if all the roads truly go to the same place and the destination rather than the path is the only thing that matters.

A simple study of the major faiths, however, quickly showed me that their doctrines, or rules for the road (or even the road itself), differ drastically. Which begs the question (on which secular philosophers and theologians agree): can two opposite realities both be true? In philosophy this is known as the law of non-contradiction. Two opposite positions are either both wrong or one is wrong, but they cannot both be right. In other words, a person can't be dead *and* alive at the same time.

As we think about all the roads to the top of the mountain, let's look at a list of the major world religions by percentage and number.

The world's twenty largest religions and their number of adherents are:

1.   Christianity (2.1 billion)
2.   Islam (1.3 billion)
3.   Nonreligious (secular/agnostic/stheist) (1.1 billion)
4.   Hinduism (900 million)
5.   Chinese traditional religion (394 million)
6.   Buddhism (376 million)
7.   Primal-indigenous (300 million)
8.   African traditional and diasporic (100 million)
9.   Sikhism (23 million)
10.   Juche (19 million)
11.   Spiritism (15 million)
12.   Judaism (14 million)
13.   Bahá'í (7 million)
14.   Jainism (4.2 million)
15.   Shinto (4 million)
16.   Cao Dai (4 million)
17.   Zoroastrianism (2.6 million)
18.   Tenrikyo (2 million)
19.   Neo-Paganism (1 million)
20.   Unitarian-Universalism (800,000)

This is where many people leave the discussion and check the spirituality box. You may think it's fine for a million people to have a million different versions of faith, but if God created this orderly universe, whose galaxies and worlds stay in place, and the world, whose sun rises every day and whose seasons come and go like clockwork, it is logical to think that he didn't allow for contradictory ways to approach him. Yes, he's mysterious and unfathomable, but surely an omnipotent and omnipresent God wouldn't allow contradictory faiths to destroy his creation in their scramble to know him.

It didn't seem probable to me that a God of love, meticulous design, and wisdom would illogically say, "Here are 25 different books with completely different foundational doctrines. In one of those books I sacrificed my son, and I say he's Lord. In the others I don't say he's Lord, but pick what you want, it's all well and fine."

So many kings and great leaders throughout the ages have decided the claims of the writers of the Bible to be true. The writers backed up their claims with miracles and consistent character. It wasn't like me waking up tomorrow and declaring, "I'm God, believe in me! I can save you!" There would be no proof. The fascinating thing about Christ is, he claimed to be God, and he gave proof through historical evidence of healings and lives being transformed.

Throughout history, plenty of people have claimed to be deity. In the last fifty years, several men have claimed they're the second coming of Jesus. As I explored various religions, I found that others have claimed to be mixtures of Muhammad, Buddha, and Shiva. Owobusobozi Bisaka, Sun Myung Moon, Inri Cristo, Shoko Asahara, and Jim Jones are a few.[3] The names didn't register on any level with me in terms of fame. The only recent example I could recall was David Koresh of the infamous Waco Branch Davidians in 1993. He, like the others, faded into history after twenty or so years; whereas Christ, after two thousand years, is still remembered, and the cross—the way in which he died—is a symbol that endures on millions of buildings and around millions of people's necks around the world. His specific narrative of hope has stood the test of time through empires, culture shifts, and generations of people, providing a reliable source of salvation amidst the storms of life.

As I looked at all the religions, I found fascinating the various programs each year at Christmastime that explored the veracity of Christ's claims. Various professors at schools like Notre Dame, Yale, and Duke, all PhDs, all referred to the Gospels as historical events. They never referred to them as legends or myths. These people have spent decades of their lives dissecting the words and narrative of the Bible. They didn't see the events as fairy-tales but as historical fact. Of course, not all saw Christ as Lord. But it adds gravity to the discussion when folks no one would claim as morons are giving polish to the metal.

So I started to see the historicity of Christianity as being true and validated. Then there's the argument that, sure, it's historical, but Christianity was created to maintain control of people. I have no doubt there are religions with that exact goal; Ron Hubbard and Scientology have been accused of this type of manipulation. Maybe Christianity was just a creation of mankind for reprehensible reasons. However, a casual read through the Gospels showed me this doesn't appear to be the intent. I'm not saying people don't misuse the message for their own purpose, but I am saying, taken at face value, to me the gospel message is a thing of beauty.

To be fair in my exploration, I wanted to assume all religions were created solely for the purpose of controlling others. If so, we throw out all religions, and we're back to asking what moral foundation do we use for guidelines? Do we just try to do our best at what society says is the way we should live? How we do know that what society determines *IS* best? Again, we have to look to something outside ourselves as a standard for measure. I needed to know if this was true. So far in my rigorous study of the Bible, everything I found showed the opposite.

Back in the year AD 50, what if a secular Israelite said to his Christ-following buddy, "You're telling me that 2,000 years from now people on the other side of the planet are going to believe in Jesus? No way!" It appears an Israelite in AD 500, 1000, or 1700 could ask the same question. The answer is, yes, a rinky-dink movement started two thousand years ago by a guy on a donkey with twelve ragamuffins formed the moral bedrock of the United States and numerous countries around the world. Remember, this movement has lasted through governments and empires rising and falling; it maintained relevance when the United States was no more than a few hundred people, and it still does now with 320 million inhabitants. Of course, all 320 million Americans are *not* followers of Christ. But no amount of clever marketing or fear tactics could keep a movement alive for two thousand years around the world, across disparate languages and cultures.

Let's circle back to the driving analogy from the beginning of the chapter. When we go to other countries, we must follow the local rules of the road. Similarly, world religions have unique foundational doctrines that all drive people forward to run a race. Correct. But if all religions are running the same race, their contradictory foundational teachings would be like trying to run a race with lanes going in completely different directions. There could be no "winner," only people meandering randomly with no finish line in sight.

As I discovered, the fact is that each religion has a unique foundational doctrine. My explanations below are by no means comprehensive. For example, I'm not spending time explaining differences between Orthodox Jews and Conservative and Reform Jews. My explanations serve as clear delineations among the major religions.

HINDUISM

God: It has three primary Gods: Brahma, who creates the universe, Vishnu, who preserves the universe, and Shiva, who destroys the universe. There are six major schools of orthodox Indian Hindu philosophy—Nyaya, Vaisheshika, Samkhya, Yoga, Mīmāṃsā, and Vedanta, and five major heterodox schools—Jain, Buddhist, Ajivika, Ajñana, and Cārvāka.

Prophets: There are not any specific prophets or founders of the faith.

Jesus: There are several varieties of Hinduism with a divergent set of views, which makes it difficult to isolate a unified set of beliefs related to Jesus. Hindus often worship many gods and goddesses and some include Jesus in their list of deities. But they don't see Jesus as the only way to God.

ISLAM

God: Muslims believe there is no God but Allah, and Muhammad is his messenger. There are five pillars of Islam. The fifth and final pillar of Islam is the pilgrimage or Hajj to the Saudi Arabian city of Mecca. All able-bodied Muslims must perform the Hajj at least once in their lifetime. There is no mention of this, nor is it required in Hinduism, Judaism, Buddhism, or Christianity.

Prophets: Muhammad is described as the final prophet from God. He listed the previous prophets and included Jesus in that list, which also includes Adam, Abraham, and Moses.

Jesus: Muslims believe Jesus performed many miracles and believe Jesus was a prophet, but they deny he is God or the son of God. While Muslims acknowledge the Second Coming, they maintain Jesus will return as a Muslim and follower of Muhammad, returning to earth to revive Islam.

BUDDHISM

God: Buddha didn't claim to be a deity. The core teachings of Buddhism are the Three Universal Truths, the Four Noble Truths, and the Noble Eightfold Path.

Prophets: Buddhism does not recognize prophets like the three Abrahamic faiths. Buddha is the central character of the religion.

Jesus: Most Buddhists acknowledge and respect the fact Jesus lived a self-sacrificial life and had compassion on those who were in spiritual need. While Jesus is seen as a wise teacher, he is not seen as divine.

JUDAISM

God: The main teachings of Judaism about God are that there is a God and there is only one God. Only God created the universe and only he controls it. Judaism also teaches that God is spiritual and not physical. Jews believe that God is one—unity: He is one whole, complete being. Rabbinic tradition includes the spirit of God, but it is not in unison with the Holy Spirit of Christian theology.

Prophets: There are major and minor prophets, not based on importance, but on the length of their books in the Hebrew Bible.

Jesus: Both ancient and modern Jews typically accept Jesus was a rabbi and popular teacher. They would deny he is the Messiah.

CHRISTIANITY

God: God exists as the Trinity: the Father, Son, and Holy Spirit. They are all equal and have unique roles.

Prophets: There are major and minor prophets in the Old Testament (OT), and then apostles and disciples in the New Testament (NT). Obviously Judaism recognizes the OT prophets, but not the apostles and disciples of the NT in the form the NT intends. Hinduism and Buddhism do not include any of the OT or NT prophets in their doctrines.

Jesus: Jesus is the son of God, *IS* God, and is the messiah come to save all of mankind. He died and was resurrected, and this event is the central doctrine of Christianity, known as salvation through the grace of Jesus Christ.

Muslims believe the Quran is unique among divine revelations as the only correct book protected by God from distortion or corruption. Christians believe Jesus Christ is the Son of God and the messiah who came to save the world, and the entire Bible is the chosen holy book. Depending on the Judaic theology, some Jews believe we are still waiting on the true messiah and that Christ does not fulfill the role.

Muslims believe that Allah is One, the only true God. To associate a partner with God (as they perceive the Christian doctrine of the Trinity to have done) is to commit the unpardonable sin of "shirk." God is absolute in his omnipotence and so wholly other, that it's impossible to have a personal relationship with him.

There are no references to Muhammad in the Christian Bible. Buddhism and Hinduism have no mention of Muhammad, nor of any of the common prophets mentioned. Buddha never claimed to be God or to be a path to God. Christianity believes Jesus lived on earth, died on the cross, and miraculously rose from the dead. Christians believe a personal relationship is the crucial element of the faith. His death and resurrection are the all-important foundational elements of Christianity. Remove it, and the entire faith is a complete farce. Without Christ's resurrection, Christians are essentially children wishing for the Easter Bunny to leave some cute little colored eggs filled with candy.

See how completely different these major religions are? While they all have overlapping moral similarities of don't steal, don't kill, and be kind to all people, their foundational truths completely contradict each other. There are fifty-plus differentiating factors between the major religions. And fifty different things cannot contradict each other and *ALL* be true. The one unique fact that distinguishes Christianity from all others is the idea of *works*. Other religions *earn* their way to heaven, hoping for God's approval; they are essentially hoping to be *good enough*. Christianity offers a free gift without any work to earn reception.

I'm by no means dismissive of the other major faiths, nor am I an expert. I appreciate that a devout Muslim will respect but not agree with Christian theology. The primary point is, what I discovered is regardless of our devotion or expertise, we cannot both be right about faiths that contradict each other.

I'll boil this down to a simple analogy. Saying that all major religions are pretty much the same is like saying *Lord of the Rings*, *Game of Thrones*, and *Star Wars* are the same movies because they're fantasies. Not at all. They each have different characters, unique themes, and distinct and unconnected endings. Yes, Marvel Comics is able to connect all their superheroes in the same universe. But we don't lump Thor and Luke Skywalker together as connected brothers. The most gifted team of writers and producers couldn't connect the dots with those three films and create a harmonious ending. Neither can we with Hinduism, Buddhism, Judaism, Christianity, and Islam. Either all are wrong, or one is right.

Questions:

1. If you have your own version of spirituality, how does it hold up when considering the history of the major religions?
2. Do you trust you have sufficient authority and evidence to claim your spirituality will last for centuries for others to study and worship?
3. How much time have you spent studying the major religions of the world, and which books and experts did you turn to as a foundation for your conclusion?

17

GOD PLAYS CHESS

"Belief is a wise wager. Granted that faith cannot be proved, what harm will come to you if you gamble on its truth and it proves false? If you gain, you gain all; if you lose, you lose nothing. Wager, then, without hesitation, that He exists."

—Blaise Pascal, *Pensées*[1]

"I have always considered 'Pascal's Wager' a questionable bet to place, since any God worth believing in would prefer an honest agnostic to a calculating hypocrite."

—Alan Dershowitz, *Letters to a Young Lawyer*

I anticipate you may be skeptical of the claims about Jesus Christ in the last chapter. You may want to pitch this book and bolt because, "Here he goes, another Bible-thumper." I understand the negatives. A personal pet peeve of mine is people who call themselves *futurists*. The definition of a futurist is someone whose brilliance is that of such super-nova luminance, they are able to predict what will happen in culture, business, or technological advancement in the next decade. I would be patient if the title were *best-guesser* or *dice-roller*, but when I have a meeting scheduled with someone with a business card titled "futurist," I begin gritting my teeth, dreading how the person will likely speak of themselves in the third person. Bible-thumpers can be the same; they have all the answers packaged in trite, pithy, Hallmark cards. I roll my eyes when someone gets preachy and holier-than-thou and uses phrases such as "God has a plan" when my life has been turned upside down.

That is our challenge. In our brief time on earth, how can we trust there is a lucid plan and an even larger entity who governs all details in our lives and in the world? The enormity is beyond our limited faculties to process—even for a *futurist* and Bible-thumper (there's a marriage made in heaven). One thing I've found helpful is looking at God as an eternal chess player. He's playing a much more serious game than us. We see in one dimension, maybe three or four moves in advance. But God is infinitely dimensional. He is *sovereign* (to use a biblical word); he's in control of all machinations. He's the ultimate CEO of the universe. We're not puppets he controls like a marionette master, but he is pushing the chess pieces around the board. He engineers the circumstances of our lives.

As the eternal chess player, he may move one piece that gives us a head cold to keep us home from work for a day. Maybe we've been overextending ourselves and don't recognize how our engine needs a break, and we need to slow down and rest. He may move another piece where we lose a job via downsizing, possibly because we've succumbed to workaholism and have been neglecting our family. The stakes often ramp up if he wants to get our attention. Maybe he allows a debilitating illness to force a person to think about mortality. This is never a one-to-one application, and how God works in each person's life is unique and mysterious.

The point is that he moves pieces that disrupt our lives. Unfortunately, our pride and obstinance require a potentially stern or painful event to occur. Much as we may be offended and despise the disruption, we may need it to get back on course. In the same way a basketball coach makes his team run extra laps for lackluster play, we need the ultimate coach to guide us back to true north. Yes, I do have regular battles in my mind where I wonder why God seems to be acting like such a dick, the same way I did with several of my coaches when I was a youngster.

God also provides wonderful blessings in the form of marriage, children, or a promotion at work. Often we recognize these blessings and give appropriate thanks. However, all too often we forget where the blessings came from and think our own ingenuity and initiative were the origin. God plays his *humility* cards to help us stay focused on what's important. I won't digress into a discussion of why God initiates challenging circumstances, and yes, of course I come close to lunacy trying to make sense of it all. I completely understand the difficulties in comprehending individual sickness and natural disaster. This was one of the strongest impediments stopping me from believing in any sort of God, let alone a God who supposedly loves us and has our best interest at heart. I encourage a deep dive into another book by Randy Alcorn called *If God Is Good*. He offers in-depth explanations of how to reconcile the tragic events we experience in life, and he does so with a gentle hand, while not offering bunnies and sunshine platitudes.

Blaise Pascal was a seventeenth-century philosopher who said that it's better to live like God exists than that he doesn't, because the reward if he exists will outweighs the risk if he doesn't. If right, we've won the lottery a million times over. If wrong, we've lost nothing; we'll end up as dirt anyway. On the flip side American lawyer Alan Dershowitz asked a brilliant question: Would God prefer someone who's honest about not drinking the Kool-Aid than someone who says they did but don't really believe? He's saying a person is a hypocrite to believe without *REALLY* believing. I see both sides.

I encourage wrestling with their ideas. I have come to the conclusion that taking a chance on Christ pays empirical dividends. In fact, I didn't have to make any sort of bet, ala Pascal. I felt like I was in a tractor beam. I wasn't looking for God. He grabbed me in a full nelson. I kicked and screamed as he dragged me into a relationship. A skeptic could say I'm biased based on my individual case. Yes, no doubt. But too many millions of people have had similar about-faces to dismiss this possibility as wishful thinking. Are there hypocrites as Dershowitz theorizes? Yep. Who knows whether those folks have knocked on the door of God or given lip service for a personal benefit, while knowing deep down they don't believe. I'm not skeptical of their disbelief, but I am making a bet in this book that a God of love will respond to a person who with integrity knocks on the door of truth.

For now, let's stick with the idea that regardless of whether we understand the circumstances of our lives, God is working in our favor. Even when circumstances provide an abundance of reasons to deny a good outcome, God supplies enough evidence of how he blesses us. Life itself is a blessing we had no control over originating; this includes the reality that most people reading this book were born in the United States. For many people in the world, a U.S. birthright is a lottery win. Having traveled extensively to third-world countries, I now realize the gift we were given by a sovereign entity. He's playing a game of chess I can't possibly fathom; but I can suspend my disbelief enough to know his movement of the pieces leads to the ultimate victory.

Questions:

1. Are you able to trust the eternal chess moves being played in your life? At what times have you thought

the game is rigged, and at other times felt a check-mate occurred from something outside yourself?

2. Does it make sense to you that God must disrupt the game of life to get your attention?

3. If God is infinite and beyond our comprehension, could it possible that he can reconcile all the minor and major catastrophes we experience or hear about in the media?

18

THE WRONG GAME

"But the thought of being a lunatic did not greatly trouble him; the horror was that he might also be wrong."

—George Orwell, *1984*

I purposely placed this chapter after a discussion of world religions. Many people have baggage from religious dogma and may throw up their hands at this point and default back to trying their best to be a good person. I empathize with you. When I read headlines about flagrant pastors or when I look at my own hypocrisy and inconsistencies of faith, I understand why people shut down any discussion or consideration of pursuing the meaning of God, let alone a relationship with the creator of the universe. Stick with me; if you've made it this far, you're already well into the journey of searching for truth.

I used to play golf as a teenager. I got to where I could shoot in the mid to low 80s. I was decent, but nowhere close to being the club pro, let alone a PGA player. In golf, there's a standard set of clubs needed to competently play the game. Let's say I never saw anyone else play or had anyone teach me, and I learned how to play the game on a deserted island that happened to have a golf course. Let's say the only instrument available to play the game was a baseball bat that floated up on the beach. Month after month and year after year I practiced and became a decent golfer... who only uses a bat and doesn't know the rules. Maybe I could achieve some level of proficiency with the bat, maybe I could shoot 90 consistently. The reality is, an average golfer could show up with a full set of clubs and likely beat me every round, especially when I was required to follow all the rules. I could try as hard as I want, and have all the talent in the world, but it wouldn't matter how great I became if I were playing the game with the wrong equipment and no rulebook. This might be the case when trying to be good enough to enter heaven. What if most people are playing the game incorrectly, competing with the improper tools, not knowing the right rules?

We're also accustomed to cultural and political gamesmanship related to class, money, and looks. You may have tried to enter a nightclub where there was a bouncer behind a velvet rope. You stood in line and waited, hopingd the bouncer thought you were cool enough to enter the establishment. I'm reminded of the classic Groucho Marx line, "I don't want to belong to any club that will accept me as a member." If heaven is even 2 percent of what Randy Alcorn claims in his book *Heaven*, we do want to be members of the club. Think of God as the ultimate doorman letting us past the velvet rope, and his game has nothing to do with being the coolest, prettiest, or richest person in line. His only requirement is us accepting an absolutely free gift. Um, yes please.

Remember my friends I mentioned early in the book, whom I asked to create their own definition of good? Another challenge we faced if we tried to create our own game and rules of being a good person was what would happen if we arrived in heaven and God said our lists were wrong. Yes, our lists had some crossover in terms of general morality. You could say our games seemed to have similar ways of scoring. But once I introduced additional items like volunteering, praying, and donating money, the lists became completely different. Or when I introduced different concepts or levels of "bad," say murder versus a misdemeanor, my friends again didn't like my position. I continued asking would they get mad at God if he had his own standards that didn't match theirs and looked similar to mine. Therein lies the problem: we're not God, but we for damn sure want him to do what we say, not vice-versa. We want to wager with the creator of the universe and hope he's fine with however we want to define how the universe works. As if he's going say, "Sure, you make the rules, I'm cool with it."

Maybe you're still convinced having your own list of good and bad qualities is good enough for entry into heaven and eternity. Are you confident you're playing the game correctly? In my experience, not one person has come up with a definitive measure for making the grade to enter heaven. It seems many people play a version of their own game with mediocre definitions of "good," and no one mentions anything about "absolute greatness"! They basically play the game hoping to be *good enough*. This makes me question whether people are playing the game incorrectly, counting on rules to a game that doesn't exist.

Questions

1. How do you know you're playing the game of life the correct way? If four people or 5,000 people agree with your version of the game, what if everyone is wrong? (Yes, the Bible could be the wrong version of the game. As an exercise for the next three months, try proving it's wrong.)

2. If you're a Muslim and required by the Quran to pray five times a day, what happens if you miss a day? What is the outcome if a devout Jew doesn't keep all 400 Levitical laws in the Old Testament? With these two faiths, is there an addendum in the religious rules for a person who fails to play the game the right way? Is there sufficient forgiveness in these Abrahamic religions?

19

IS GOD A DONKEY OR AN ELEPHANT?

*"My concern is not whether God is on our side; my
greatest concern is to be on God's side, for God is
always right."*

—Abraham Lincoln

I don't want to offend anyone by taking political sides. I
include this discussion only because politics create a massive barrier for people to consider Christ, and as I began
my journey with him I struggled with the political angle.
I've had plenty of friends give me the Heisman because
they associate Christianity with the Republican party.
People are fed up with a partisan Congress with each party
seeming to cauterize the other at every turn. At the writing
of this book, there are multiple movements with passionate advocates including #MeToo, Black Lives Matter, open

borders, and free trade. The issues have been divisive, and the discourse is rarely civil. One of the debates that has pushed tempers to the brink is the fact that 65 percent of evangelicals voted for President Trump. Many of those voters expressed their position by saying Trump was the lesser of two evils, with Democratic candidate Hillary Clinton seen as the devil incarnate. Some evangelical voters said Trump appeared to be closer to their conservative values than Clinton, particularly on the issue of abortion.

Many agnostics and secularists criticized Christians as being hypocritical. How could Christians vote for the twice-divorced billionaire who once a week shows little regard for decorum, and doesn't appear to read a Bible, based on his declaration of "two Corinthians 3:17" at Liberty University during the run-up to the election? That's not how someone knowledgeable of basic biblical nomenclature would describe that specific book of the Bible.

Let me level the playing field to make the more salient point. Not only is Trump the worst president in the history of the United States, so were Ronald Reagan, Harry Truman, Franklin Delano Roosevelt, Abraham Lincoln, *and* George Washington. Uh, what was that? Yep, it's guaranteed you can find haters of every president in every century. Yes, maybe I'm a raving madman hopped up on caffeine and clearly in need of a lucidity pill. Or you can grasp the reality that no president is perfect, and most people pick their favorite the same way they pick a sports team. Lastly, don't let any leader's victories or egregious behavior color your perception of God. The best people you know, men and women, are hypocritical and broken. No one is perfect.

The best position from my vantage is to say that all of us, whether Republican or Democrat, are incredibly flawed humans. No side is more right or wrong than the other, and, yes, this position too will be criticized as people line up to compare past presidents and candidates. You'll find a large number of Christians who emphatically state Christ's values are Republican, and an equally high number who say he would vote as a Democrat if he were an American citizen.

What is absolutely true is that both sides of the political aisle have impaired people who are a mix of good and bad leadership. Same as all of us, they're a gumbo of contradictions. The beautiful thing is, Christ loves people on both sides of the aisle, plus the independents who have given the finger to each party. Christ had positions on moral issues, which are ultimately political issues, and those positions are universally focused on helping all people. He got angry at the establishment for being hypocritical posers and told others they need to stop sinning, not waste their talents, and get in the game to help their fellow man. By far he said all of us are defective people, and we need help at the highest and deepest level.

The same way the Bible is not a history of how electricity and wind works, it's also not an exposé on how to vote politically. It's a love letter from God to mankind about a broken relationship, an extended version of Romeo and

Juliet as he woos mankind back to ultimate intimacy. For me, someone new to the Bible, that was a mind-blowing revelation. Wow! God is in love with people and wants to engage with *me*?

Yes, if you are a Christ follower, your vote should be informed first and foremost from scripture. But you'll get in the weeds quickly if you try to pigeonhole God into any political party. It's like calling Apple a nice little mom-and-pop shop.

The main thing to focus on is don't let politics, natural disasters, or a crappy church stop you from considering Christ in your pursuit of truth. I often tell people to focus on the red words of the Gospels. That's Christ speaking to people. The layers of life start to fall into place after you confront and process the red words.

Questions:

1. Have right-wing conservatism and the surrounding political issues caused you to dismiss Christ?
2. Have you read the red in the Gospels? Compare the red words of Christ with all political parties.
3. Can you name a politician who is uniformly regarded as the greatest person known to mankind? Did he or she have no faults, no imperfections… and walked on water?

20

NATURAL PRESERVATIVES INCLUDED

"What an astonishing thing a book is," marveled Sagan. "It's a flat object made from a tree with flexible parts on which are imprinted lots of funny dark squiggles. But one glance at it and you're inside the mind of another person, maybe somebody dead for thousands of years. Across the millennia, an author is speaking clearly and silently inside your head, directly to you."

—Carl Sagan

I mentioned before that many people say the Bible was written by men and therefore can't be trusted. Basically, there's a pervasive point of view that the Bible is a 3,400-year-old version of the telephone game, where people pass along everchanging stories. In other word, after centuries of "whispering" in each other's ears, the stories have been embellished and distorted to an indistinguishable outcome from the original. And now with all the claims of *fake news,* nothing can be trusted. I understand and empathize. I used to ask myself: what could this fabricated book possibly have to do with my life today?

One thing that grabbed my attention was when I looked at the book as a love letter from God instead of as some dreadful rule book designed to take away all fun. Before I walked down scholarly lane, I needed to know I could believe this book was accurate.

I'm a huge fan of Terry Gross's epic radio program *Fresh Air.* Several times she has interviewed Bart Erhman, a professor at the University of North Carolina at Chapel Hill. An expert on the New Testament and the history of early Christianity, he's written or edited a ton of books, five of which were on the *New York Times* bestseller list. Dr. Ehrman is soft-spoken and comes across as a cordial professor who has cracked the code on the conspiracy of the Bible. He's plenty smart as a textual critic, and at first blush he certainly seems to be a profound authority on the Bible.

> Bart Ehrman has used his prestige as a text critic to give the impression to lay people that the text of the New Testament is terribly corrupted and uncertain. He wrote a book called *Misquoting Jesus* in which he gives the impression to lay people that we really don't know what the original New Testament said because, as it has been copied over

the years, so many thousands and thousands and thousands of variants have crept into the manuscripts that it is just uncertain what the original text read. An interviewer who assumed the Bible was accurate, once asked Dr. Ehrman what he thought the text of the New Testament originally really said. Ehrman replied, 'Well, it says pretty much what we have today – what it says now.' The interviewer was utterly confused. He said, 'I thought it was all corrupted.' And Ehrman said 'We've been able to reestablish the text of the New Testament as textual scholars.'[1]

The scholarly Bart Ehrman knows that the text of the New Testament has been established to 99 percent accuracy. That is to say, the original wording of the New Testament is now established to about 99 percent. So the degree of uncertainty of the text of the New Testament is only about 1 percent. There are about 138,000 Greek words in the New Testament. Of these, only about 1,400 are uncertain today. 99 percent are established with real certainty.[2]

In other words, there are scholars who have debunked Dr. Ehrman's positions. Dr. Ehrman knows, and when pressed, admits that the text of the New Testament is 99 percent accurate. So even atheist historians know the Bible is historically accurate. Keep in mind we don't doubt whether George Washington existed. We don't doubt historical views on Napoleon or Alexander the Great. We actually have more copies of the Bible in relation to other historical books. In the old days, manuscripts were written on a papery substance that disintegrated quickly, so people had to keep making copies by hand in order to preserve the books. And the oldest copies we have are sometimes centuries younger than when they were first written. Plato's *The Republic,* for example, was first written around 380 BC, but the earliest copies we have are dated AD 900. That's thirteen hundred years later! And there are only seven copies in existence.

Caesar's *Gallic Wars* were written between 100 and 44 BC. The copies we have today are dated one thousand years after he wrote it. We have only ten copies.

When it comes to the New Testament, written between 50 and 100 AD, we have more than five thousand copies. All are dated to within fifty to 225 years of their original writing. Furthermore, when it came to scripture, scribes (monks) were meticulous in their copying of original manuscripts. They checked and rechecked their work, to make sure it perfectly matched. "What the New Testament writers originally wrote is preserved better than any other ancient manuscript. We can be more certain of what we read about Jesus' life and words, than we are certain of the writings of Caesar, Plato, Aristotle and Homer."[3]

This blew me away. And then I found out that the integration of scripture is profound. The Bible has more than forty authors spanning roughly 1,600 years. The writers were a ragamuffin mix through the centuries: laymen, fishermen, farmers, philosophers, statesmen, and poets. Keep in mind they lived in different centuries and on three separate continents. Yet with all this diversity, they wrote with continuity. Imagine gathering three of your friends and asking them to write a book together... but not telling them individually that two others are participating... *AND* not explaining the plot and subject matter. What chance would they have of creating a book with any level of flow and linear progression? I'd say zero. By the same token, could a global conspiracy lasting sixteen centuries continue pulling our chain without eventually dying out? Again, there's a teeny-ass chance, unless there's some real meat to the content.

Chuck Colson was a Nixon lawyer who was caught up in the Watergate scandal. He makes a good point:

> "I know the resurrection is a fact, and Watergate proved it to me. How? Because 12 men testified they had seen Jesus raised from the dead, then they proclaimed that truth for 40 years, never once denying it. Every man was beaten, tortured, stoned and put in prison. They would not have endured that if it weren't true. Watergate embroiled 12 of the most powerful men in the world-and they couldn't keep a lie for three weeks. You're telling me 12 apostles could keep a lie for 40 years? Absolutely impossible."[14]

Yes, I hear you, what's the damn point? Reputable scholars and historians, whether religious or not, don't doubt the veracity of the Bible. Which means, as you consider multiple truths in relation to death, go hard at proving it wrong. Dig, scrap, fight, scream, go all in.

Getting back to the love letter: I had viewed the Bible as a rule book designed to be the buzzkill of all things cool. I also doubted it because there was no mention of the history of dinosaurs, earthquakes, astronauts, magnesium, jellybeans, mustard, or orcas. In my ignorance, I had no clue of the purpose of the book. It's like trying to read a desktop instruction manual and hoping it will move me to tears like Cormac McCarthy's *The Road*. I had the wrong mindset for the narrative. The Bible is an extended multilayered poem from God to mankind, not a history of the world. God uses his own creation as authors to call us back to him. The relationship has been broken, yet God cares about us the way we care for a lover in the deepest part of our soul. Except multiply his love exponentially, to the point of losing a child, *on purpose*, as a means to buy us back with a ransom. Astounding.

The gospel of John says, "No one can come to me unless the Father who sent me draws them, and I will raise them up at the last day" (John 6:44 (NIV). This is one of those verses that forces a decision. Again, there's no wiggle room.

C. S. Lewis in *Mere Christianity* pushes the envelope about Christ:

> I am trying here to prevent anyone saying the really foolish thing that people often say about Him: I'm

ready to accept Jesus as a great moral teacher, but I don't accept his claim to be God. That is the one thing we must not say. A man who was merely a man and said the sort of things Jesus said would not be a great moral teacher. He would either be a lunatic—on the level with the man who says he is a poached egg—or else he would be the Devil of Hell. You must make your choice. Either this man was, and is, the Son of God, or else a madman or something worse. You can shut him up for a fool, you can spit at him and kill him as a demon or you can fall at his feet and call him Lord and God, but let us not come with any patronizing nonsense about his being a great human teacher. He has not left that open to us. He did not intend to.[2]

That's a mighty blow to our thinking. We have one of three choices. If we say Christ is only a great teacher and nothing more, we're calling him a liar. Why? Because he didn't claim to only be a great teacher, plus he performed countless miracles to prove he's anything but a human teacher. The second choice is he's a total nutcase, like Lewis says, on the level with someone claiming to be a poached egg. Or, lastly, he is exactly who he claims, Lord of the universe and savior of all mankind. For me, the revelation of that question was an ass-kicking. I kept rationalizing and thought I cracked the code, then I would sit for a minute and realize, dammit, I'm still landing at liar or lunatic. I guess there could a fourth option where we say Christ is irrelevant, a person could dismiss him outright. Maybe. But it sure seems like the person who proves Christ is worthy of dismissal would themselves be elevated to equally lofty status.

I've mentioned David Koresh of the Branch Davidians, from the tragic Waco event in the mid-1990s. He claimed to be God, and we quickly deduced he was crazy. Christ also claimed to be God, same as David Koresh. But we reset our calendars based on his birth. Even if people don't agree with Christ being both God and man, not many people view his teachings as those of a lunatic. The third option is he's exactly who he claims and what scripture says: Lord of the universe who created everything, including us.

I understand if you're saying, come on, there's no way I'm buying this! That's what I thought. But if you say no to believing in Christ, you double back to the discussion of the scales of good and bad. You have to hope they tip in your favor.

While we may not want to believe it, God very well may have spelled out exactly what a person needs to do to enter heaven. Remember everything we've discussed so far:

1. Five religions can't all be true if they contradict each other.
2. God is in charge. God cares for us more than we comprehend.
3. There is statistical significance that his written word is the Bible.

But it's *man*-made. Here's my follow-up question to the hundreds of people who have shot back at me with, "You know the Bible was written by men?" Yep, everyone is well-aware of that fact. The more challenging question is, *why* did they write it? Was it a conspiracy? Did various people over 1,600 years decide to randomly make stuff up about God? Possibly. Or maybe God told them what to write through intuition and prayer. The more I thought about it, the more the last answer made more sense. The Bible has history, it's considered authoritative, it has veracity. It has historical figures we know existed. The Bible will be discussed fifty, 100, or 500 years from now. This is my provocation to anyone reading this book: ask tougher questions. Go deeper. Compare other religious texts. Authors of the Bible were considered prophets, disciples, and apostles. It's withstood the test of time, weathered the challenges of critics and religious scholars. Yes, compare Islam, Judaism and Christianity; read the various outspoken atheists making waves in the media. If God wants you to know truth, he will show you the way.

Questions:

1. How would you answer the question of Christ being either liar, lunatic, or Lord as he claims?
2. If the Bible is false, what person or group started the conspiracy? If it was the church, how did the church originate, if based on a complete falsity? How have people been able to keep the conspiracy

alive through the centuries? Are the reasons sound and verifiable from experts?

3. If God is pursuing you to fix and secure a relationship, and his purpose is to help you through worry, sickness, heartache and death, is the idea worth exploring?

21

PASSION FOR YOUR FAMILY AND FRIENDS

"The true soldier fights not because he hates what is in front of him, but because he loves what is behind him."

—G. K. Chesterton

My dad was faithful to my mom for fifty-nine years; he raised my sister and me in a stable household. He was a provider, he was devoted to my mom, and he cared for her every need. He was a good father, measured by how he taught me valuable lessons as my coach in the sports I played growing up. However, for twenty years of my adult life as an adult, he was dismissive of my faith and repeatedly said he believed in a moral code instead of Christ. He watched lots of TV and played golf a minimum of three times a week. While he was a regular at my and his grandkids' athletic events, which was wonderful devotion, he never volunteered with charities, he never mentioned prayer, and it was not his personality to ask about my personal life. If looking through a lens of good and bad measures, by most accounts he would land on the good side. He had no lawsuits, no record of burned bridges with friends, but he also was not an epic philanthropist who impacted the community. Will I see my father in heaven since he was relatively good on most days?

For more than fifteen years after the truths of the Bible became real to me, I encouraged or argued with my parents on the importance of thinking about heaven. I sent multipage letters, extended text messages, and provocative books for them to read to help them think beyond their opinion, which was often dismissive. Two years before my dad died, we had a very difficult conversation where I asked if he cared about his family being together in heaven. I worded it as, "Let's say heaven truly exists, lasts forever, and is devoid of pain and suffering. You would want all your family together for eternity, yes? If it were available, you'd want us all there, right?"

He shrugged and said, "No, doesn't really matter to me." I kept rewording it to ensure he understood. He did, and three different times the answer stayed the same. He never got past saying, "Doesn't matter to me." It's difficult to articulate how painful this was to hear. It was unfathomable to me how I could begin to comprehend such a statement. I eventually forgave him and came to realize we can't make a person believe or care, even if we use family as the motivator.

Three weeks before he died I asked him again if he would like to accept Christ as his savior. By this time, his dementia was increasing, and I hope it didn't cloud his decision, but he said yes. I'm counting on Christ to take the decision of a mustard seed as enough for my dad to be in heaven. I have peace about it, and I am not tossing and turning at 3:00 a.m., which I attribute to God providing comfort instead of worry.

Here's another example of redemption. A close friend and former business partner of mine murdered a drug dealer—his own drug dealer, actually. He served twenty-two years in prison, "accepted Christ" while in "time out," as he calls it, and now impacts lives in the name of Christ, who, according to scripture, still loves him regardless of his past crime. I find it beautiful that my friend, who could be categorized as a *bad* person, is absolutely allowed into heaven.

So is it fair for my dad to be allowed into an eternally perfect place, when he said he doesn't care whether his family is there or not? If a person doesn't believe in God, or, like my dad, spends the majority of their life never giving God the time of day, it may be difficult to believe the slate can so easily be made clean so they can come join the party. Or is it right that my friend who killed a man could be forgiven? Is time behind bars enough penance for a lost life? Some would say yes, others might write him off. Tricky stuff for sure when I try to evaluate on the scales of justice.

This is why I found Christ to be so beautiful and amazing. People can ignore him their entire lives—like my dad—and, at the last moment, choose to thank him for dying for their pride and ignorance. And he says, "Yes, be with me forever." Or a person can end up going down a path that leads to a terrible outcome—like my friend who served time in prison. Again Christ says, "Yes, spend all of eternity with me."

I'm a gargantuan fan of Anthony Bourdain. He rocked it at the highest level of go hard or go home. I heard him say twice on his shows that he wasn't religious and considered himself an atheist. One of my friends, when developing their definition of a good person, said, "A person needs to inspire others." Bourdain clearly inspired people; he opened our eyes to different countries, people, food, and music. Through his passionate and gritty lens, he showed us the world as a spectacular adventure to be lived out. Tragically, he took his own life in 2018. When I heard the news, I was sitting in a coffee shop. "Damn!" I exclaimed loud enough for several patrons to turn and stare. As I write this, I'm struggling with how to respectfully discuss a taboo subject like suicide. And my deepest pain rests here: what happens to a person who dies and claims to be an atheist who doesn't believe in God? I hate asking, and I wish I didn't question an atheist's ultimate destination.

With Bourdain, many Twitter tributes mentioned "RIP in the great kitchen in the sky." While I agreed with the sentiment and pain of losing such a brilliant mind, I struggled to understand how an atheist can end up in a

place that appears to be governed by an entity an atheist fundamentally believes does not exist. Yes, I would
love to say we all end up at a peaceful destination. But
the question circles back to: who is the gatekeeper of the
next haven after this life? A friend read an early draft of
this section and didn't jive with my idea that Bourdain
didn't believe in a God who could have relieved his pain.
She said, "It's like saying what he should have reached for
was no more real or viable than reaching for a magic pony
who would whisk him away." A great point, and so painful to hear and comprehend. Yes, why didn't God step in
and relieve Bourdain's pain? I didn't know him; I don't
know if he cried out to a deity and never got a response.
Intellectually I know what scripture says: God is always
pursuing us and wants to know us. Do I believe that in
my heart? In fits and spurts. Quite often I think God's
love language is Russian, and all I know is Japanese. I have
to dig past my angry emotions and decide what role God
plays in tragic deaths, and what role all of us—Bourdain
included—play when we make decisions to harm ourselves
and others. If we choose to not believe in God, are we in
effect cutting off our lifeline to the thing that sustains us?
Pain and tragedy seem to be the biggest barriers to belief
in God. And the answer of God giving us free will doesn't
fully placate and soothe my angst. We want him to stop us
from hurting ourselves. But like a parent struggling as they
see their child fall through life and receive physical and
mental wounds, God allows us to make harmful decisions,
consequences be damned. Oftentimes I hate the reality,

but then I recognize how living like a puppet would be no life at all.

Without the concept of grace, how would God judge such complicated positions as my dad or my friend or Anthony Bourdain? How many people are similarly complicated: good on some days, and in other moments, totally jacked up with their irreconcilable ideas and pasts? Simplistic scales of good and bad seem pedestrian at best, and woefully prejudiced at worst. The beauty of forgiving grace shines through as a free gift to all people. The definition is spectacular to comprehend, bringing the promise of erasing all our mistakes individually, and restoring all 7.6 billion lives on this planet to full absolution. Stunning. My mind is officially warped in awe.

Questions

1. Evaluate your family. Do you find a mixed bag of sometimes upstanding character, and days, months, or years of character issues that cause grumbling?
2. Are there specific issues you struggle with when considering how Christ forgives all people of all their mistakes?
3. Do you think you're more deserving than most people to be in heaven? Why?

22

GOD SENDS PEOPLE TO HELL?

"For the past three hundred years men have been pointing out how similar Jesus Christ's teachings are to other good teachings. We have to remember that Christianity, if it is not a supernatural miracle, is a sham."

—Oswald Chambers, *The Highest Good*

This has been the toughest chapter to articulate. I tried placing it in multiple locations during the writing of the book, including the crapper. At first, I thought I should call it "Triple-Super-Duper Bullshit!" or "Mike Lyon is Warped... His Fictitious Children Ugly... Santa Claus Hates Him!"

When considering belief in a loving God, a major deterrent is the perception of God as a punisher of people.

We view him as stalking us from above with a quiver of lightning bolts, ready to strike us down for every mistake large or small. This idea culminates with a position of not wanting to worship a God who sends people to hell. He must be cruel and mean for damning a person to a horrible place for all eternity. I agree. I would not believe in or worship a God who would do such a thing.

This is not going to be a popular, but here comes a grenade. The theological answer is that people *CHOOSE* to go to hell. I can see your hands flying up in the air, saying, "No way! Who would choose hell?" The logic looks like this in linear progression.

- Death is inevitable.
- Good is not good enough.
- There is an intelligent designer/creator.
- Not all religions are the same.
- God is a loving boss, and we're not.
- One religion offers a way out of our guilt.
- We know that the Bible is accurate and true.
- We all have a choice to believe Christ or not.
- God gives us exactly what we choose, and we spend eternity with or without him.

You may have heard the phrase, "We live behind the 'buts.'" It means that how we actually feel is found after the conjunction *but*. For example, "Back in the day I was one of the best basketball players in the history of Texas! … *but* I didn't make all-district because my coach didn't like my attitude." Or, "Yes, I love me some Italian food! … *but* not pizza, fettuccine, ravioli, or marinara sauce." In other words, we tell on ourselves with the "buts." This is where the truth rests for us as we state our positions.

In a discussion of God or faith, a case of the buts might look like this: "I definitely believe in God… *but* I don't believe in organized religion." Or, "Yes, I believe God is in charge of the universe… *but* why is there so much pain in this world?" And the big one: "Wait, I want to be with God and my family and friends in eternity, *BUT* I don't want to believe in Christ." This response misses the point of God sacrificing his son for your every past, present, and future mistake. How easy is it to accept a free gift? You may think there are strings attached, and I understand the trepidation. However, any perceived rules or guidelines introduced to you after the decision are designed to give you the best life. Think of the principles and applications as a loving parent who tells their child not to play in the street. The child thinks the parent is being malicious for not allowing him complete freedom, when the parent is actually protecting his loved one. Or go back to our boss analogy: even the best company will likely have attributes or requirements you may not agree with, yet you still work there for the overall good.

But I'm not doing justice to how wonderful it is to believe in and have a relationship with God. It's not drudgery; it's not Sisyphean in effort. It's the complete opposite. There's a deep, undeniable comfort that resides in your soul. Yes, plenty of days will still be unbearably rough.

But think of him as the ultimate safety net, the perfect mapmaker guiding your life. No matter how far off in the jungle you venture, he's still there looking out for you.

In my conversations, the biggest *but* for most people is the idea of pain and suffering. If God is so powerful *AND* loving, why does he allow millions of people to endure such agony. The answer isn't simple and is one for the ages, which countless theologians have poured over. I've mentioned Randy Alcorn's book *If God Is Good* as a fantastic exploration of the subject. For the sake of this book, I encourage you to keep in mind that Christianity includes a God who knows pain and suffering, He dealt with betrayal and the apathy of friends. Do I rest on that knowledge every time I struggle? Not by a long-shot. I drop several f-bombs in frustrated prayer to grasp any level of contentment. *BUT* I do trust we have a God who promises to reconcile all the horrors in this world. On some days, that's enough juice to keep me going.

Here's how John Eldredge in his daily newsletter from October 26, 2018, explained the idea of choosing hell:

> Jesus' heart of love is not diminished by the fact that some people will actually choose hell over surrendering to God. He weeps over it. He warns, urges, pleads, performs miracles. As they nail him to the timbers, he says, 'Father, forgive them, for they know do not know what they are doing' (Luke 23:34).

The exclusivity of Christ is often what creates a barrier and is what many people find crazy-ass offensive. Let's look at this notion. First off, if I were God of the universe, it seems logical that I would try to be as clear and seamless as possible. If I give people five different religions to choose from, I run into the issue I discuss in chapter 16, "All Religions Are the Same": all religions have foundational doctrines that contradict each other, so they cannot all be true. Therefore, it seems God would provide a single pathway to keep it easy for us to comprehend. God always kept it simple, but scripture also speaks to an enemy known as the devil, who complicates truth with his lies. Eldredge goes on to say:

> To make sure we understand this, what He is saying is that He alone (Christ) is the means to heaven. No one comes to the one true God except through Him. Offensive as the claim may be, we still have to deal with it. Either it is arrogant, or it is true.

That's a fascinating way to phrase the conundrum: it's either arrogant or true. I think with our limited faculties yet ginormous hubris, we do choose to think God must be arrogant to be so exclusive. But again, is it arrogance, or is *simple* a better word?

One of my closest friends says he just doesn't believe in Christ, and he's comfortable with his decision. He says if he ends up in hell, he'll live with it. I understand how God is mysterious and how a decision for Christ is difficult; there's a fear of the unknown. We're betting on something we can't see, touch, smell, or hear. We read about an event that supposedly took place two thousand years ago, and we don't see the relevance to our lives today. Plus we know plenty of jackass Christians who are hypocrites and worse. We see leaders, politicians, and our neighbor down the street who are the exact opposite of what Christ represents. Yep-yep-yep, I get it. However, the magnitude of hell is often misinterpreted as a slight downgrade only, like the equivalent of hanging out in a dive bar. Sure, all the booze is not top shelf, and the jukebox doesn't have any Beatles or Stones, the booths smell like old cigarettes, but hey, it ain't all bad. Lots of my friends are here.

If only that were true. Correct, I've never been to hell, nor do I know anyone who's visited. But I do know that the descriptions offered in the Bible and other literature are terrifying. All the worst words we use to articulate the conditions won't do justice for how dreadful it is.

Guaranteed there are people reading my nine-step progression who feel I made towering leaps to draw my conclusion. Again, I empathize. For example, let's say I encouraged you to make a discerned effort to seek truth in your life. You opened your mind, heart, and hands and said, "Ok universe/God/Peter Pan, I WANT TO KNOW TRUTH!" The friggin' frustrating narrative of the Bible says we're incapable of seeing the truth until God grabs us in a headlock and shows us. Even then we kick and scream like dictators in childcare. Whuh? Scratching your head? Me too. As much as I want to kick the Bible to the curb twice on Tuesday, and doubly so on Friday, it does accurately depict what happened to me. I wasn't looking for truth, and I was quite damn happy with the one that was working for me. In hindsight, I understand exactly what scripture says about us essentially wandering in darkness until God turns on the light switch. More head scratching and the question of, "Great, what are we supposed to do if no light is happening?" My best answer is to keep knocking on the door, plus life will help create breadcrumbs for the path. How? Because in this world you will get kicked, you will bleed, and you will want some sort of balm to help. Booze, sex, money, and travel will only go so far to fill the emptiness; and the knock may be a gentle tap, or you might pound the door with a sledgehammer.

I'm not interested in using religion as a deterrent. In fact, I rarely use the word *religion*. Some people do respond to boogeyman tactics of fire and brimstone, but this ain't that book. Live for today and please do appreciate the beauty of life in all facets. Try to make each day count, love your spouse, love your children, laugh at great comedy, be a friend who encourages and listens well. But do remember we all have a finality in this life. It's a fact, and one from which we can't hide.

Questions:

1. What roadblocks do you have in accepting God's free gift to you? What if the perceived rules or things you might give up have nothing to do with reality?

2. When you think of heaven, is is inspiring enough to pursue entrance for you, your family, and your friends? When you think of the possibility of hell, is it alarming enough to ensure you don't end up there?

3. What are your *buts* with God, religion, and Christ?

4. Is it possible that God could reconcile all the tragedies of this life by creating a perfect heaven with no pain and suffering? What if all unfair things ultimately are made fair in the long run? Could that knowledge give you hope?

23

WHAT'S YOUR CHOICE?

*"As much money and life as you could want!
The two things most human beings would choose
above all—the trouble is, humans do have a knack
of choosing precisely those things that are worst
for them."*

—J. K. Rowling, *Harry Potter and the
Sorcerer's Stone*

In the opening scene in David Mamet's film *Glengarry Glen
Ross,* Alec Baldwin rips into a group of weathered salesmen
who answer to his uptown bosses. The entire sequence is
eight minutes give or take, but the impact is jaw-dropping
and visceral. In his soliloquy, Baldwin asks at a fever pitch,
"Have you *MADE* your decision for Christ?"

Have you? There is no gray area or *buts.* There's no box
to check that says, "Sure, I think he's a good guy... *BUT* I

don't really believe in him as God." No option exists for, "Follow Christ… *BUT* Hinduism, Judaism, Buddhism, and Islam are okay too." I'll say it again: a devout Hindu, Jew, or Muslim will preach the exact same thing I am—that their idea of God is the only true option. This is why I said don't waste time and energy on your own definition of spirituality. Study the major world religions and see where you land. You'll find excellent guidance and life maxims in all the major religions. But we're talking about the be-all end-all of life after death in this world. This is by far the most important decision you'll ever make. Any family, spouse, or career decision is a distant second.

Because of the millions of changed lives who point directly to Jesus Christ, those same millions believe he is exactly who he claims to be. I'm one of those people. I thought the whole thing was unmitigated bullshit, and I thought exactly as you do: "I can make up my own God, and he, she, it or whatever will be fine with *MY* definition." Then God came to me—without my searching—and dramatically changed my life on October 22, 1999. The details are irrelevant other than on that night, a strange sense of calm and peace came over me, without my asking. I had never experienced something like it, and I wondered if it was romantic love (some of the irrelevant details). It wasn't, and I felt like I had zero choice in the matter. I've met people all over the world who've had similar experiences. There's a consistency to all believers' stories: they went from non-belief to a 100 percent reversal. The decision didn't fill their lives with bunnies and sunshine, but they knew unequivocally that Christ is exactly who he claims to be. My conversion included exploration of Abrahamic faiths of Islam and Judaism and a basic study of Buddhism and Hinduism. I'm no expert on those major faiths; hell, I'm still trying to understand Christianity and how it applies to every facet of my life. But I do know that a logical God would not provide contradictory truths.

My question for all people who do not know Christ or believe in him is this: if his claims of a *free* gift of forgiveness include eternal life with all our family and friends (who believe in him), wouldn't it be worth exploring? In heaven I want to meet people who may have been influenced by this book in their decision for Christ. Maybe it's three people, maybe ten, whatever number is fine by me. I want us to enjoy each other and laugh together over wonderful meals for 10,000 and 100,000 years. Life and death is a very real and serious business, and we need to be demanding in our thinking and decisions.

Please keep in mind, IF Christ is a complete fabrication… IF he's nothing more than wishing Bigfoot exists… Then he is—by a million miles—the most mammoth hoodwink and crime against humanity, in the history of the world. Bar none, nothing else comes close.

So what do we do with all this? For one, congratulations, you just finished a book on a topic that polite society says we're not supposed to discuss. My encouragement is to keep living life with the goal of impacting your fellow man. Inspire others by serving those in need, open the door for strangers, say, "Yes, sir," and, "No, ma'am," and strive to listen well and encourage often. All these tangible goals make us solid people each day we live.

But go deeper. All you have to do is take a step toward believing Jesus died for all your mistakes at no cost to you. Even if you're not 100 percent sure of that reality, the decision is the same. And that's it; no strings attached. After I knew Christ had grabbed me, I still had questions. It wasn't as if I immediately understood everything about the Bible. You can still question plenty of things about God and scripture, but the only decision you have to make is to ask Christ into your life and believe he paid the price for all those goofs in your life. You don't have to speak any exact wording; you simply need to surrender to the idea of Christ being your new manager. Please know, having a new manager doesn't make life one big lottery ticket. Don't expect a gravy train that only stops for more candy and cash. Life will still be a bitch on plenty of days. In fact, you'll often want to fire your boss because he appears to be clueless and cold.

And now here's your challenge. If you claim to be spiritual or agnostic, if you're a casually religious follower of one of the major faiths, or if you think all organized religion is the worst thing ever perpetrated on mankind, I encourage you to take five minutes each of the next seven days, praying or meditating, it doesn't matter what you call it. Grab coffee, tea, a cold Dr Pepper, whatever helps you chill and block out the noise. Say something similar along the lines of what is below on each of those seven days. Doesn't matter if you miss a day, and it's irrelevant if it's two minutes instead of five. The point is be purposeful. Block out the anxiety to get your day going; the to-dos can wait for this teeny smidgen of time. Take notes on what thoughts come to mind, pay attention to what happens during the seven days. Does a friend randomly call to discuss life's big issues? Does an article on faith randomly pop up in your newsfeed? Follow the breadcrumbs and see where they take you. Ask friends what they think. If you wanna go big and dive deep, grab a copy of C. S. Lewis's *Mere Christianity* or a modern apologetic discourse like *The Reason for God* by NYC-based Tim Keller. Check out books by former atheist and legal editor of the *Chicago Tribune*, Lee Strobel, and pick up Randy Alcorn's book *Heaven*. If you're edgy and like some whisky and sass with your truth, dive into Anne Lamott. She's gold. If you want to dig deeper into science and creationism, grab a copy of Francis Collins's *The Language of God*. Definitely read atheist Sam Harris's *Letter to a Christian Nation* and *The End of Faith* and Richard Dawkins's *The God Delusion*. See if their arguments against God hold their salt.

During those seven days, try something like this:

"God, if you're real, I want to know you. I'm not sure what I believe about you or heaven, or the idea that I'm not good enough for entrance. Show me the path. If this guy Jesus is relevant, if he's real, if he can help me and make my life better, I'm all ears. Right now I think it's all horseshit, but I do want to know truth. Show me the way. I've heard

the word 'grace' before, but it means nothing to me
now. Help me understand."

There's no magic. No hypnotism, no lighting of candles or
waiting for angels to sing. Knock on the door and see if
God responds. Will your life change overnight? Possibly.
I've had friends who prayed the prayer, and they've experienced some pretty freaky stuff. I'm not God, so I
can't guarantee he flips the lightswitch. I know he wants
to know you in a bigger way than the closest friends and
most intimate lovers. It may be similar to exercise, where a
change occurs after months of strenuous sweat.

While searching for truth, keep your fingers out of
your ears and have your radar up. This I guarantee: if you
ask God to show you truth, he will show up with a love and
grace you'll appreciate more than the best vacation, best
food, best friend, and, yes—the best sex you've ever had.

Enjoy the journey.

Questions:

1. After several days of the prayer, have you noticed
   any interesting conversations, a new intuition, or
   news articles *randomly* showing up?
2. What perceptions, opinions, and worldviews have
   changed for you after days, weeks, or months of
   seeking truth?
3. What are your biggest barriers to believing in Jesus
   Christ? What makes you call bullshit on the entire

idea? Pray about it. Yes, I'm serious, no bullshit. Wrestle with your issues in a prayer similar to the one in this chapter. Then keep your radar up for answers that arrive through friends and *random* content that might show up in a newsfeed.

4. Do you know people who once were atheists, but who now believe? Seek them out and ask the tough questions.

APPENDIX

Sample Conversations

When researching this book, I spoke with several close friends and acquaintances. Often the discussion played out like the dialogues below. I offer this as a framework for what you may experience with your family and friends. The names have been changed so we can affably enjoy beers and cigars in the future.

Conversation 1

Friend: "Nobody really knows what the lists are for good and bad. God would've told us."

Me: "Boom, there's the kicker. Maybe God did tell us the proper path and plan through his words in the Bible?"

Friend: "It can't be a MAN-made doctrine."

Me: "The Bible is man-made, no question. It's also historically accurate and not some fictitious book. Yes, plenty of folks don't believe Christ died and rose again, but the book is still a historical document. Many historians consider it to be *THE* most important historical book. The argument of man-made boils down to the question of whether all us Christians (and Jews to a certain extent) have bought into the biggest lie and fraud in the history of the world. If false, this is a conspiracy of proportions a thousand times bigger than the JFK assassination. If a lie, then Christ has duped millions of people for centuries! If you want to live by a self-created list and present it to God as more authoritative than what he may have inspired men and women to write in the Bible, go for it. Also keep in mind that any list or doctrine we create outside the Bible is *ALSO man-made*, just sayin'."

Conversation 2

Friend: "Is your moral compass just? I believe instinctually, most people have a moral compass and can determine what's right and wrong. By sticking to the compass, we can walk down a righteous path. Doesn't mean you have to be perfect, but it means you can be just. Examples, you see an injustice happening, do you speak up? Or when you see someone like President Trump who doesn't appear to exude Christian principles. Shouldn't evangelicals speak up? You see someone in need, do you help?"

Me: "Yes, certainly speak up when you see injustice. But how do you determine whose moral compass is just? Yes, most people do have a moral compass, but we know for a fact that plenty of people have a compass that's WAY off, and most of us have one with cracks in it. Whose compass is right? I agree regarding Trump not walking the walk, and I believe evangelicals made a poor choice in justifying him. He's nowhere close to the definition of servant-leader. There are millions who believe in Christ who think Trump is the furthest thing from Christ in the Bible. It sounds like you recognize there is a standard of morality. I encourage you to find the right one that comes from a higher authority. If not, then ten people, one hundred people, or one thousand people can make up anything that works for them."

Conversation 3

Friend: "I think God judges each person on individual criteria, and being spiritual is fine."

Me: "What is the criteria? You can't cherry-pick from the Bible, because it says nothing along the lines of 'do your best to be a good person.' I'm trying to understand how a person who is spiritual can believe in something they made up on their own. How do they know it's right? More importantly, how do they know God the creator is okay with their one-page definition?"

Conversation 4

Me: "What happens if a person has been to prison? Or committed a minor felony? Are they disqualified from the good list, and ultimately don't make the cut for heaven?"

Friend: "Society shuns them."

Me: "My question pertains to not living up to a definitive list needed for entrance into heaven. Yes, society shuns you, but possibly God too if you chose the wrong list."

Friend: "I get that idea, but I want you to push yourself and strip religion away from this, too. How do we derive purpose and become a good person today?"

Me: "Can we strip away religion? Actually, I do strip away the stereotype of religion. But I don't think we can remove God. It's like taking away a car engine and hoping you can still drive across the country."

Me: "What about people who have committed adultery?"

Friend: "They have to live with themselves eventually."

Me: "I'm asking is there a measurable metric for TOO much adultery? Or too much of anything bad? Plenty of folks seem to be fine with ongoing adultery, ongoing lying. They live with themselves with no sweat. Won't they end up in front of God hoping they had enough other good stuff to outweigh their adultery or (insert bad things)?"

Friend: "Yes, but I think eventually their lives crash on themselves. Whether it's self-inflicted or societal."

Me: "Your list is slightly different than Bill's, slightly different than Bob's, slightly different than Fred's. What if God has a different list than everyone else's? Does he or she or it simply say in a mob voice, 'Forget about it. Ay, your list is good. Bada-bing.' In other words, does the list we create supersede what God says?"

Friend: "Do the best you can while you're here. Society and your conscience determine if you can come back from your mistakes."

Me: "Doing the best you can be while we're here is fine, but still ambiguous. You still haven't given tangible metrics. One hundred percent of us have to deal with death. None of us has a choice in whether we believe in death. Death doesn't care whether you believe in it, it's absolute. It's sort of like saying, 'I don't believe in heat of the sun.' The sun doesn't care, it's still going to cook you!"

Friend: "I've told you many times, I don't live for heaven. I live for today and my world."

My friend is focused on consequences of our choices and mistakes on this side of death. And that's important, no doubt. Yes to everything he says: in this life my life will crash in on itself if I constantly lie and cheat... Yes, society will shun me... Yes, I will likely have a difficult time sleeping at night ("having to live with myself"). And while society and your conscience have some say in whether we can come back from our mistakes, individuals and society *CANNOT* provide ultimate cover. Yes, we should live for each day and fully engage and max out those twenty-four hours. But eternity is far more important, so contemplate it. Let's say we pencil out our lives on this side of eternity compared to what happens after. We quickly see how our forty, fifty, or ninety years are a speck of lead compared to an ongoing line of eternity. Therefore, the latter should be our focus, because eternity lasts forever.

Conversation 5

Friend: "What if the Bible is man-made and God actually wrote our lists through each of us? What if our time on earth is so we can come together and constantly work to understand those 'lists' and inspire each other to make this world a better place? What if those lists look more like the Muslim, Jew, Buddhist, and Hindu lists than each religion's books?"

This response is after the fact, I didn't reply directly to him. Yes, God did orchestrate and write the Bible through people. I also agree he wrote a plan for good works for each of us. I wish it were so that people did come together to understand each other's values and worldviews. A quick look at various Facebook posts says there's a significant number of people NOT trying to understand each other. They're just hatin' away. I don't agree with the idea that a person's individual list would deviate from the religious book they view as their map for life. In other words, if my list of good things didn't look like what the Bible says, there would be contradictions. My life wouldn't match scripture, which would seem to say I'm not living out the loving mandates of the Bible.

Conversation 6

Friend: "Do you leave the world better than you found it? This is broad, but I think it's part of of the continuum of life. Are you raising your children with the same moral character and selflessness you've wanted to exemplify in your own life? What role in the environment are you playing? Are you wasteful? Revengeful? Or selfish?"

Me: "This was another area I found myself fumbling in fear. Sometimes my moral character is solid, but I've had my moments where my jealousy and anger would not qualify as a morally solid person. Regarding the environment, in the last few years I started recycling plastic, but there's plenty of times I still throw a water bottle in my regular trash. Am I wasteful? Definitely when compared to people living in Haiti and other third-world countries where resources are scarce."

Conversation 7

Me: "All religions say God is the source of why we WANT to do good. The fact that the majority of people don't just start killing people speaks to the idea of an objective morality that isn't arbitrary to each person."

Friend: "Wow, that's a horrible argument. Do atheists kill more people than those abiding by a religion? Not everyone needs a God to tell them how to act."

Me: "Correct. But they do need a God to enter heaven. An atheist would say they don't need God to be moral and inspire people and to give back. Absolutely correct. But there's still the same question of what is the motivation for those things. Plus, the atheist WILL need God to access and enter heaven. Saying they don't believe in

God isn't a sufficient response. He's provided enough evidence of his existence; taking a pass on belief will not give an atheist resolution. It's not like there's some other awesome, cool place for those people who didn't want to believe in God. This circles back to the question of who's the boss and who has authority for access to heaven."

Conversation 8

Friend: "This is where the 'don't be a dick' portion of my thoughts go. Some people are just negative in thought, spirit, and mind, and that causes a darkness in a person. That can manifest itself in a lot of ways. Lying, murder, abandonment, unfaithfulness just to name a few."

Me: "I've been a dick plenty of times. I know lots of negative people who, when I dig a little bit, had horrific family backgrounds. Do they get a pass on being a dick because their family of origin dramatically impacted their personality? What if I'm unfaithful to my husband or wife? Do unfaithful people get into heaven? Again, it seems important to know what the criteria are so I can act accordingly and not screw up, right?"

Conversation 9

Friend: "Selfless deeds toward others, without need of anything in return. Does your heart just give without consequence? Is there always a catch? Giving freely and selflessly seems to be a must in order to get in. Be a force for good."

Me: "I asked for specific metrics. What kind of selfless deeds? Give with your heart without consequence. Great, I like it. But what about when I'm selfish with my giving? If we're honest, we often expect something in return. How much does a person have to give freely? Is once a year enough? We measure everything on this side of heaven, so wouldn't God measure with specific benchmarks? In other words, how much inspiration is required? Force of what kind of good? Can it be any kind of force I think is good? What if someone else thinks it's bad, or not a worthy definition? Is once a month enough, or once every ten years? What if I inspire people occasionally, but I piss people off frequently? Again, see how this is impossible to measure?"

Conversation 10

Friend: "Having a spiritual base. Feeling connected to some type of higher being, whatever that may be, and figuring out what those principles are and living them. Are you true to them? Do they keep you grounded in your own morality?"

Me: "A spiritual base like the Branch Davidians in Waco? They felt connected to a higher being. Again, you say 'whatever that may be,' so I guess I can believe anything as long as I'm serious with my belief? Hitler and Stalin are the standards for believing fervently in something that was wrong. We know because we have a moral compass for a benchmark. What about

Planned Parenthood? What if I exclude people of a certain race or belief? I bet you're going to say, 'No, it has to be fair and just.' Yes, I agree, but who determines 'fair and just'? What if I create a religion that says killing bad people will give me one hundred virgins in heaven? If we say they're wrong, we have to base it on the correct idea of right. It's the same with Christianity. If we say Christianity excludes gay people (which it doesn't, by the way), and we think that's wrong, we have to find the true definition of right and wrong."

(Just a head's up, Christianity says *ALL* of us have made mistakes, both straight, gay, bi, black, and white. It says none of us are perfect, and God has forgiven us for all our mistakes.)

Conversation 11

Friend: "When defining good, do you inspire others? Are you a beacon of light for other people? Do they view you as a force of good? By doing all the things listed above, I can't help but think that rubs off on other individuals, and means you are sharing in the light of the world."

Me: "These are all admirable goals on how to live your life. But you're missing my point. It's not a question of whether a person should *try* to live out these qualities. The question is about how to measure the qualities. I hope the distinction is clear."

Conversation 12

Me: "I keep asking, how much do I have to give? Are you talking time and money? I think you understand my point of anything ambiguous is not a metric. To be a good person do I have to inspire people once a year? More? Twice a month? How much money do I have to donate?"

Friend: "Yep, and 10 percent sounds like an arbitrary bullshit number designed by corporations to justify their pay."

I appreciate my friend's sentiments. He's referencing the biblical concept of tithing 10 percent. That sounds arbitrary, and, drilling deeper, his bigger concern is the veracity of scripture itself (I can say this because he's told me about his skepticism) and whether churches are simply ensuring their staffs secure a salary. The tithe is somewhat of an arbitrary number; however, if a person does believe scripture, the point God is making is for us to give back money he gave us in the first place. And 10 percent is a small amount, and we can live on and enjoy the other 90 percent. If a person disagrees and pushes back on the 10 percent, fine, pick any number, but do it.

Regarding church staff salaries, there definitely are organizations who may not be using their funds beyond a paycheck. It's unfortunate but true. At the same time, the vast majority of churches are trying to serve the needs of their congregations and communities. The salaries are normally not excessive and are justified by effective results.

The fascinating thing about tithing is that statistics have shown most Americans tithe, at best, maybe only 3 to 4 percent. So even for Christians, they don't live up to this measure.

Which again segues to my point of what happens if God made a firm rule that a person *MUST* tithe 10 percent or 20 percent or 3 percent of their income every year? What if there was a mandate for giving? We would immediately be in an uproar, saying life's not fair, the economy is down... I lost my job... I had to pay for my kid's college, etc.

Closing Conversation

Friend: "These are the things I think you need to do to 'get in' to heaven. I'm just not a believer that it's all that complicated. And whether you're Christian, Muslim, Jewish, Hindu, etcetera, this doesn't seem to be the barometer by which we should be measured."

I agree with my friend, making a decision for Christ is not complicated. Really, it's not. However, this book is designed to show how futile it is to try to come up with a list of good things everyone can agree on AND actually measure. Live by the golden rule? Sure, but I know for a fact I haven't. Invest myself in others and my community? Yes, but I'm nowhere close to what Mother Teresa did, or even the two nuns I served with in Guatemala.

For final clarity, I'm not saying I avoid this side of life and am *ONLY* waiting for heaven. Some believers live in a crippling place of avoidance and fear. I am saying the idea of living for today and MY world should be measured against eternity. This world is fleeting; we know for a fact the metric for this life is likely only forty to ninty years, with some tragedies and anomalies on either book-end.

You may think, "Good for you, you have a special calling." Fair enough. I'm certain people do have a special calling for unique ministry, Mother Teresa for example. But all people can help others think about the inevitable, which means all have a special calling.

The Story Needs to Be Told Again

Christianity promises a relationship with the God of the universe who became a man. This man, Jesus Christ, came to save us from ourselves and to erase all the past, current, and future mistakes in our lives. This is called the gift of grace. He died for all our mistakes at ZERO cost to us. We can either choose to accept this or not. Very few historians doubt the historical veracity of scripture; very few people doubt Christ truly lived. Set aside the idea of trying to be a good person. Instead, try accepting this free gift from God and see what happens.

NOTES

CHAPTER 2 Fade to Black

1. C.S. Lewis. *Mere Christianity*. HarperSanFrancisco, 2009.

2. M. Scott Peck. *The Road Less Traveled*. Simon & Schuster, 2002.

CHAPTER 4 God? We Don't Need No Stinking God!

1. A.W. Tozer. *Tozer on Christian Leadership*. Moody Publishers, 2015.

2. Randy Alcorn, *Heaven*, (Tyndale House Publishers, 2004), 443.

3. Pew Research Center, Global Attitudes and Trends, 2007 Views of Religion and Morality

CHAPTER 6 The Bad

1. "The All-Time Worst People in History," Ranker, https://www.ranker.com/crowdranked-list/the-all-time-worst-people-in-history.

2. Ibid.
3. Ibid.
4. Ibid.
5. Ibid.

CHAPTER 7 The Ugly

1. Richard Cohen, "What if the FBI had succeeded in exposing Martin Luther King Jr.?", *Washington Post*, November 17, 2014, https://www.washingtonpost.com/opinions/richard-cohen-the-medias-self-indulgent-examination-of-character/2014/11/17/7072ad96-6e8e-11e4-ad12-3734c461eab6_story.html.

2. Madhusree Mukerjee, *Churchill's Secret War*. Basic Books, 2010.

3. Ramachandra Guha, *Gandhi Before India*. Knopf, 2014.

4. Denise Grady, "A Glow in the Dark, and a Lesson in Scientific Peril," *New York Times*, October 6, 1998, https://www.nytimes.com/1998/10/06/science/a-glow-in-the-dark-and-a-lesson-in-scientific-peril.html.

5. Maud Newton, "Flannery O'Connor's Complex, Flawed Character," *NPR*, March 31, 2009, https://www.npr.org/templates/story/story.php?storyId=102500858.

6. Edna Medford, Ph.D., "Lincoln's Evolving Racial Views," Rutherford B. Hayes Presidential Library & Museums, February 14, 2010, https://www.rbhayes.org/hayes/lincoln-s-evolving-racial-views/.

7. Paul Finkelman, "The Monster of Monticello," *New York Times*, November 30, 2012, https://www.nytimes.com/2012/12/01/opinion/the-real-thomas-jefferson.html.

8. Walter Isaacson, *Einstein: His Life and Universe*. Simon & Schuster, 2007.

CHAPTER 9 Spiritual Not Religious

1. Pankaj Mishra, "The Last Dalai Lama?," *New York Times*, December 6, 2015, https://www.nytimes.com/2015/12/06/magazine/the-last-dalai-lama.html.
2. "Principal Commitments," DalaiLama.com, https://www.dalailama.com/the-dalai-lama/biography-and-daily-life/three-main-commitments.
3. "Buddhism at a Glance," BBC.com, November 17, 2009, http://www.bbc.co.uk/religion/religions/buddhism/ataglance/glance.shtml.
4. "Principal Commitments," DalaiLama.com, https://www.dalailama.com/the-dalai-lama/biography-and-daily-life/three-main-commitments.
5. "Principal Commitments," DalaiLama.com, https://www.dalailama.com/the-dalai-lama/biography-and-daily-life/three-main-commitments.

CHAPTER 10 Alternative Spirituality

1. *The Bitter Southerner*, 2018
2. "Is Buddhism a Philosophy or a Religion?" *Huffington Post*, December 6, 2016

CHAPTER 13 The Watch Builds Itself

1. Mike Wall, "The Big Bang: What Really Happened at Our Universe's Birth?", Space.com, October 21, 2011, https://www.space.com/13347-big-bang-origins-universe-birth.html.

2. Anonymous, "Aristotle (384-322 B.C.E.)," Internet Encyclopedia of Philosophy, 2009, https://www.iep.utm.edu/aristotl/.

3. Preston T. Kin, *Thomas Hobbes: Critical Assessments*, Volume 1, (Taylor & Francis, 1993), 59.

4. Isaac Disraeli(1835). *Curiosities of Literature*. W. Pearson & Company. p. 371

5. Anonymous, "Aristotle (384-322 B.C.E.)," Internet Encyclopedia of Philosophy, 2009, https://www.iep.utm.edu/aristotl/.

CHAPTER 15 Who's the Real Boss?

1. "Basketball: A Love Story." ESPN, 2018.

CHAPTER 20 Natural Preservatives Included

1. "Is There Historical Evidence for the Resurrection of Jesus?" College of the Holy Cross, Worcester, Massachusetts, March 28, 2006, http://www.holy-cross.edu/sites/default/files/migration/files/resurrection-debate-transcript_1.pdf.

2. Richard Rajkumar, "A Beginners Guide to Understand and Answer Dr. Bart Ehrman," Christian Apologetics Alliance, August 18, 2016, http://christianapologeticsalliance.com/2016/08/18/a-beginners-guide-to-understand-and-answer-dr-bart-ehrman/.

3. Geisler, Norman L. *Baker Encyclopedia of Christian Apologetics*. Grand Rapids: Baker, 1998.

4. Marjorie Hyer, "Colson Preaches That Watergate Proves the Bible," *Washington Post*, September 28, 1983, https://www.washingtonpost.com/archive/local/1983/09/28/colson-preaches-that-watergate-proves-the-bible/e4978ba1-795b-44ed-b9e8-2cfe90e6e2d2/.

To help continue your journey, try these:

1. *The Reason for God* – Tim Keller
2. *Mere Christianity* – C. S. Lewis
3. *Blue Like Jazz* – Donald Miller
4. *Heaven* – Randy Alcorn
5. *If God Is Good* – Randy Alcorn
6. *The Ragamuffin Gospel* – Brennan Manning
7. *Abba's Child* – Brennan Manning

And these:

1. *The God Delusion* – Richard Dawkins
2. *Letter to a Christian Nation* – Sam Harris
3. *Why I Am Not a Christian* – Bertrand Russell
4. *God, No!* – Penn Jillette

artistic lyon

www.artisticlyon.com

Mike Lyon ran away from home on his Big Wheel at five years old. This first adventure led to his adult wanderlust and future discussions of faith with friends and strangers. Now that he's all grow'd up, his writing balances work as an entrepreneur, visual artist, and how to navigate life as a Jesus freak—while distancing himself from modern "worship" music. His weekly blog is sprinkled with doses of amazing startups, people busting ass for others, and a curation of art, film, and music.

As a serial entrepreneur, having spent 20+ years with various startups in technology and content, he's been a director-producer, and recently began accepting commissions again from his previous career as a visual artist. He also teaches boxing, which one of his friends refers to as "jazz hands" since participants only crush bags and not each other. He's led or been a part of multiple humanitarian aid trips to Haiti, Nicaragua, Guatemala, Cuba, El Salvador, Africa, and India.

A proud sixth-generation Texan, his favorite proteins are Chimay and Maredsous Belgian Ales, and Rocky Patel cigars, which contribute to his tangential threads. He never turns the channel when *Goodfellas*, *GlenGarry GlenRoss*, *The Outlaw Josey Wales*, *Sicario*, or *The Mind of a Chef* are on the telly.

37996441R00122

Made in the USA
San Bernardino, CA
05 June 2019